PRAISE FOR
NICE GIRLS DON'T GET RICH

"A fresh look at how women *think* about money . . . deals with the *real* reasons women have so much difficulty with their finances. I wish [I had] it before I made so many of the mistakes she discusses."
—Barbara Stanny, author of *Prince Charming Isn't Coming: How Women Get Smart About Money* and *Secrets of Six-Figure Women*

"Explains the mixed messages women get about money . . . Tells how women can take charge of their financial lives."
—*More* magazine

"The guide you need to turn dreams into reality. Learn to think rich and discover all the wonderful things that are possible."
—Gail Evans, author of *Play Like a Man, Win Like a Woman* and *She Wins, You Win*

"Upbeat, breezy."
—*USA Today*

"Tips on how to approach financial matters with confidence and savvy."
—*Aptos Times* (Santa Cruz, CA)

"Practical advice . . . enlivened with client stories and personal anecdotes."
—*Booklist*

Also by **Lois P. Frankel, PhD**

STOP SABOTAGING YOUR CAREER
8 Proven Strategies to Succeed–In Spite of Yourself

SEE JANE LEAD
99 Ways for Women to Take Charge at Work

NICE GIRLS DON'T GET THE CORNER OFFICE
101 Unconscious Mistakes Women Make That Sabotage Their Careers

KINDLING THE SPIRIT
Acts of Kindness and Words of Courage for Women

WOMEN, ANGER AND DEPRESSION
Strategies for Self-Empowerment

NICE GIRLS DON'T GET RICH

75 Avoidable Mistakes Women Make with Money

Lois P. Frankel, PhD

BUSINESS PLUS

NEW YORK   BOSTON

Business Plus
Hachette Book Group USA
237 Park Avenue
New York, NY 10017

Visit our Web site at www.HachetteBookGroupUSA.com

Printed in the United States of America

Originally published in hardcover by Hachette Book Group USA.

First Trade Edition: April 2008
10 9 8 7 6 5 4 3 2 1

Business Plus is an imprint of Grand Central Publishing.
The Business Plus name and logo are trademarks of Hachette Book Group USA, Inc.

The Library of Congress has catalogued the hardcover edition as follows:

Frankel, Lois P.
    Nice girls don't get rich : 75 avoidable mistakes women make with money / Lois P. Frankel.—1st edition
        p. cm.
    Includes bibliographical references.
    ISBN 0-446-57709-X
        1. Women—Finance, Personal. 2. Wealth—Psychological aspects. 3. Assertiveness (Psychology) 4. Sex role—Economic aspects. I. Title.

HG179.F7 2005
332.024'0082—dc22   2004027900

ISBN 978-0-446-69472-8 (pbk.)

Book design by Giorgetta Bell McRee

This book is dedicated to every woman who works too hard, earns too little, and never seems to get ahead financially. I hope that within these pages you find the courage and wisdom needed to take whatever action is required to lead a rich life—however you choose to define it.

Acknowledgments

There are so many people I want to thank for their help with this book. I counted on old friends, new friends, and colleagues around the world to fill me in on the nuances of financial thinking—and they did. We so casually say, "I couldn't have done it without you," but in this case it's true!

- Larry Kirshbaum, Jamie Raab, Diana Baroni, Chris Dao, Joy Saverino, Leila Porteous, Les Pockell, Penina Sacks, Rebecca Oliver, and all of the other people at Warner Books who helped to make *Nice Girls Don't Get the Corner Office* a national best seller: Your expertise in your respective fields is evident in all that you do, and you're the best team a writer could ever ask for.
- Bob Silverstein for being not only a wonderful literary agent but such a good friend and sage adviser
- Dr. Pam Erhardt for continuing to be my muse and for her assistance with the data collection and analysis
- Dr. Kim Finger for being a terrific sounding board, editor, colleague, and friend
- Katherine Wimmer for so patiently, thoroughly, and cheerfully responding to my myriad questions and for providing outstanding suggestions based on her extensive experience as a financial consultant
- Joe Lumarda for his help writing the sections on charitable giving

- Karen Blanchard and Maureen Kerrigan for their on-the-mark suggestions as well as for taking the time to educate me
- Cheryl Bouchard for her insights on women and real estate
- Barbara Stanny for sharing her personal experiences and insights into women and money
- Elaine Gregory and the rest of the "lunch ladies" for taking time to share with me their expertise and experiences working with women and money
- Karen Flannery for so thoroughly and thoughtfully reviewing my manuscript and providing me with new ideas for getting rich
- Anne Fisher for her generosity of spirit and support of my writing
- Mia Anderson, Lieke Sulaiman, Ranti, and Itje Suryono for helping to get my questions distributed to women around the world
- Kathleen Booth for feeding me a perpetual stream of relevant information and ideas
- All of you who took the time to share your messages and mistakes via phone, e-mail, and personal interactions

If I've left anyone out—and at the risk of being called a "nice girl"—I apologize. No one's contribution was too small to mention.

Contents

Chapter Four   *Spending Your Money Wisely*   83

Chapter Five   *Learning Money Basics*   125

Chapter Six   *Saving and Investing for Future Wealth*   143

Chapter Seven   *Maximizing Your Financial Potential at Work*   185

Chapter Eight *Playing It Smart with Your Money* 219

Chapter Nine *Resources* 253

Introduction

From birth to age eighteen a girl needs good parents. From eighteen to thirty-five she needs good looks. From thirty-five to fifty-five she needs a good personality. From fifty-five on she needs cash.

SOPHIE TUCKER

When my editor at Warner Books and I first started talking about writing a book that would illuminate the many mistakes women make on the road to financial independence and ways to correct them, I was hesitant. There were already so many books on the market designed to help women accumulate the level of wealth they wanted. When I mentioned the idea to one journalist at the *Wall Street Journal*, she groaned, "Not another book to teach women how to negotiate!" Then it dawned on me. If there are so many books available to help women achieve their financial goals, then why do significantly more women than men live below the poverty line? Why do women between the ages of forty-five and fifty-four earn 28 percent less than their male counterparts? Why aren't women getting their fair share of the world's wealth? And most important, why aren't women following the great advice contained in all these other bo

Because a woman's relationship with money is as comple

the other relationships in her life. And this is what makes *Nice Girls Don't Get Rich* different. This is not just a book about financial *planning*. It's also a book about financial *thinking*. It's about how women, stuck in old patterns of socialized behaviors and thinking, get in their own way of accumulating the wealth needed to live their lives richly—in all ways. It's not because we earn only seventy-seven cents on the dollar as compared with men, and it's not because we don't sit in corner offices. Those are symptoms, not causes. Women don't earn as much because they are given conflicting messages throughout their lives—beginning when they are girls—about doing good and doing well. All of the financial planning books in the world won't help someone who is walking the tightrope between intellectually knowing she should be more concerned with financial security and emotionally feeling stretched about how to achieve it and still be effective in her socialized role as a nurturer, caretaker, protector, and helpmate. But a book that combines financial thinking with financial planning will—and that's why I decided to write this book.

The title of my last book, *Nice Girls Don't Get the Corner Office: 101 Unconscious Mistakes Women Make That Sabotage Their Careers*, raised a lot of eyebrows and caused much conjecture when it arrived on the best-seller lists. The most common media question I was asked, particularly by men and with a bit of sarcasm, was, "Are you saying you can't be nice and make it in business?" That's when I knew the person hadn't read the book. If he had, he would know that while it's true women can't afford to be nice to the point of being pushovers, the emphasis in that title, and this one, is less on the word *nice* and more on the word *girls*. For what gets women in trouble when it comes to getting and keeping the job they want or accumulating the portfolio they need to live financially independent lives is the tendency to act like the "nice girls" they were taught to be in childhood as opposed to acting like intelligent, capable, deserving adult *women*.

With the help of my colleague Dr. Pam Erhardt, I researched the early childhood messages women receive about money and the mistakes they make along the path to creating financial independence. I was surprised to find that our original hypothesis, that little girls receive significantly different messages about money than little boys, didn't prove true. In fact, the majority of the people we spoke to or corresponded with heard all the right messages:

- "Save for a rainy day."
- "Don't spend more than you have."
- "Create your own financial independence."
- "Methodically track and watch your money."
- "Plan now for your retirement."

On the other hand, they also heard a few messages that most little boys never hear:

- "It's just as easy to marry rich as it is to marry poor."
- "Men know more about money than you do."
- "Money doesn't buy you happiness."
- "Talking about money is crass."
- "It's better to do good than be rich."
- "Girls just aren't good at math."

Herein lies the rub. The past several decades have opened new windows of opportunity for women. Although the playing field is still not even, a woman can at least be on the field—if not the star quarterback. What hasn't changed, however, is what I write about in *Nice Girls Don't Get the Corner Office*. Women have been reluctantly invited to join the old-boys' club but told not to act like the other members if they want to maintain that membership. The perception is that role-appropriate behavior for women still involves being less assertive, direct, and competitive than their male counterparts. Even women (or especially women) who grow up in egalitarian households where they are told they can become anything they want to be and are just as good as the boy sitting next to them in class find that in the real world there is subtle pressure to conform to the cultural norms of female behavior.

After polling hundreds of women around the world and hearing stories such as the ones contained in this book, it became abundantly clear that *many of the characteristics that make women uniquely feminine are the very same behaviors that prevent them from becoming financially independent.* In many ways the greatest gifts women bring to society are, ironically, the ones that cause them to act in ways counter to their own best interests. Even if they don't hear it from their parents, young girls are still bombarded with societal messages that imply their well-being is contingent upon acting in certain stereotypical ways such as being polite, soft-spoken, compliant, relationship-oriented, and, in some cases, allowing their hard-earned incomes to be mismanaged so as not to offend someone's ego. When a woman earns her own income or inherits wealth, there is often a conflict with the expectation that she will ultimately be a mom, dutiful wife, caretaker for elderly parents, *and* independent. It's a juggling act that's difficult at best and impossible to achieve at worst. But don't let this discourage you. I also asked all kinds of experts for suggestions about how women can become financially empowered, and they responded with plenty of advice to help you lead a rich life. This advice, combined with my own based on my personal research, observations, experiences, and practices, makes *Nice Girls Don't Get Rich* a practical tool kit you can use to build your financial foundation.

When I read a book that gives me advice, I want to know the qualifications of the writer. I've already said I'm not a financial planner, but rather a business consultant, author, executive coach, and licensed psychotherapist. So in the spirit of what I suggest you do more of—talk about money—I'll model the way. I come from a family of modest means, and, perhaps like you, I was taught the importance of hard work but wasn't given the guidance I needed to leverage that into a wealthy lifestyle. Nonetheless, using the definition of *rich* contained later in this book and by applying many of the coaching tips imparted herein, I can legitimately (and with much humility) say that I am now rich. I have acquired the amount of money needed to make decisions and live my life free from financial concerns. My portfolio ranks among the top 5 percent of American women with savings. With the exception of a $25,000 pretax inheritance I received when my mother passed away, I earned it myself and, with the help of a capable financial consultant, manage it myself as well. I hope you know that I share this not to impress you, but to impart the message that if I can do it, so can you.

What this book will *not* do is provide you with a blueprint for financial planning—but it *will* help you to develop your own. My belief is that you must first understand why you act as you do before you can change your behavior. My goal is to increase your consciousness so that in turn you can take the hundreds of coaching tips provided and put them to immediate and good use. Just as you can't lose twenty pounds in a week, you can't become financially independent overnight. Use the self-assessment inventory in chapter 1 to determine the areas that are the greatest impediments to your financial success. Then focus on taking two or three tips from each of those sections and incorporate them into your daily life. Most important, make a commitment to yourself to take charge of your financial well-being. Once you do that, you'll be on your way to creating the abundance that you've worked hard for and deserve.

NICE GIRLS DON'T GET RICH

Chapter One

Women and Wealth

Women have been so brainwashed by the destructive female culture that taught them to associate money with sin, evil and everything crude, that it would take an entire book to disentangle the subconscious fears and incredible fantasies that the simple noun "money" evokes in most women.

BETTY LEHAN HARRAGAN,
Games Mother Never Taught You

Women and money. What a complex relationship. We bemoan the fact that we don't have enough of it. We don't save as much as we know we should. And we too often rely on others to manage it for us. Despite the fact that in childhood most of us get all the right messages about the importance of being financially independent, we do all the wrong things when it comes to accumulating the amount of wealth we need to be truly financially independent. Why? Because throughout our lives we're given multiple, often conflicting, messages. On the one hand, we're taught about the value of money and the need to spend and save it wisely. On the other, we're implicitly or explicitly taught that it's equally important to be kind, nurturing, and collaborative; that our real roles revolve less around money and more around relationships.

This double bind causes little girls to limit their interest in acquiring wealth and ultimately their capacity to acquire it. They don't aspire to get rich, they can't see themselves as rich, or they reduce their opportunities to get rich. As a result, they frequently lack the skills needed to create wealth. Getting rich requires you to do two things: financial planning and financial thinking. If you're like most women, you don't "think" rich—and if you don't *think* rich, you certainly don't consciously engage in behaviors that will contribute to *getting* rich. The point at which you call yourself rich is determined by your values, your lifestyle, and your risk tolerance. It's not determined by someone else's definition, needs, or expectations of you. Being rich is about having the ability to live your life abundantly—however *you* define abundance.

Although I realize that life can be rich in many different ways, for the purposes of this book when I use the term *rich*, I refer to the acquisition of financial wealth. Most of us already know that one can be rich in love, work, family, and so on. You don't need another book to tell you that. Defining *rich* in financial terms is another thing. The actual number, the point at which you consider yourself rich, is something only you can decide. Most of us will never be as wealthy as the people on *Forbes* magazine's annual list of the richest people in the world. Yet you may aspire to more than you currently have. Therefore, throughout this book when I use the term *rich*, I am referring to *the ability to live your life as you want to free from financial constraints.*

Speaking with women around the world about getting rich, I got the distinct feeling they were uncomfortable talking about money. It was as if *rich* was a dirty four-letter word. Whereas a woman may be called a "rich bitch," there are no similarly pejorative terms to describe a man. And Lord knows we avoid the b-word even more than we avoid talking about money! It doesn't seem to matter if you're twenty-five or fifty-five. As a woman you are less likely to focus on methods for becoming rich and more likely to focus on "doing good."

Having been raised as a typical "girl," I spent the first half of my adult life believing that doing good and doing well were mutually exclusive. Whereas my two brothers were encouraged to pursue college degrees that would lead to high-paying professions, I was encouraged to go into a helping field—preferably teaching so that I could be home with my hypothetical children during summer vacations. While I was working as a clerk in the radiology department of the local hospital during high school, my mother (the director of nursing at this same hospital) was introducing my younger brother to doctors at the hospital and encouraging him to become a physician. Although I worked my way through master's and doctoral degree programs, I only recently discovered that my mother offered to pay for my younger brother's graduate education if he would consider becoming a lawyer. Is it any wonder that both my brothers became independently wealthy at a far earlier age than I did? While they were thinking about making money, I was thinking about "doing good."

"Nice girls" don't get rich in large part because of the social messages they receive when they are growing up:

- Money is power, and most little girls are not taught to be powerful—they're taught to be "nice."
- Girls are socialized to be caretakers, nurturers, and accommodators in society—not necessarily breadwinners.
- As child bearers and caretakers women often work jobs discontinuously and are penalized for it. Alternatively, they're

put on something demeaningly referred to as "the mommy track."

- Women are more likely to spend their income on their children and the household, whereas men are more likely to be prudent about investing.
- Women are reluctant to ask for wages, perks, or raises reflective of the value they add to their organizations because they're not sure they "deserve" it.

Need I go on? It is abundantly clear that women don't get rich because (1) we don't envision ourselves getting rich, (2) we are more concerned with playing our social roles in a way that others consider appropriate, and (3) we don't develop the skills needed to make wise financial decisions. Does this mean we can't acquire wealth on our own? No! *It means that what you focus on is what you get, and it's time to focus on getting rich.* Just as in my previous book getting the "corner office" was simply a metaphor for achieving your professional goals, being rich is a metaphor for living the life you want to live free from concerns about money. It's not the amount of money you have that matters, it's the ability to act with independence that defines a rich life. And you will never have it if you don't start *thinking and acting* like a rich person.

Given these parameters, a woman who owns her own home free and clear, does work that she loves, and knows she has enough money to live comfortably for the rest of her life could be considered rich. She would be no less (or more) rich than a woman who lives in a home with a $500,000 mortgage, has $3 million in the bank, works so she can afford to travel, and wouldn't be worried if she were to be laid off tomorrow. What point would that be for you? Envision yourself living that lifestyle. If it's not where you are now, then this book was written for you.

WHY AREN'T *YOU* RICH?

I've been asking women around the world about why they don't have the amount of money they require to feel comfortable making the decisions needed to live their lives free from concerns about money. More specifically, I asked them to finish this sentence: "I would be rich today if I had . . ." I phrased it that way so they would share the behaviors they ignored early in their lives. Here are just a few of the responses I heard:

- "If I had taken risks and not procrastinated." A sixty-three-year-old executive from Paramount Pictures.
- "If I had a better understanding and appreciation for the value of creating a savings account from the start of my career thirty-six years ago." A fifty-year-old administrative assistant.
- "If I had not stepped aside, walked away, or ignored being taken financial advantage of. Not worried so much about being seen as too aggressive or unprofessional." A fifty-three-year-old professional services manager.
- "If I had been more assertive." A forty-eight-year-old artist.
- "If I had dared to take high-risk chances, which I didn't take because I had to juggle between raising a family and my career." A forty-three-year-old accountant.
- "If I had kept my life simple—not moved to a big house with a big overhead and a lot of maintenance." A forty-nine-year-old executive with Prudential Securities.
- "If I had not been afraid of the stock market and invested ten years ago." A fifty-five-year-old independent graphics consultant.
- "If I had utilized my potential to the fullest and been more proactive in planning my future and not depended on

someone else to actualize my hopes and dreams." A sixty-year-old real estate agent.

- "If I had not listened so closely to the advice that my father told me when I was young that I would inherit all that I would ever eventually need." A sixty-year-old diversity consultant.
- "If I had someone who told me that I could aspire to being rich." A forty-three-year-old dental assistant.
- "If I had done things that I really love to do." A forty-three-year-old business consultant.

If you can relate to any one of these messages, you're not alone. The reasons why women aren't as rich as they'd like to be are as varied as the women themselves. Sometimes it's the messages they received in childhood about money. Other times it's because of social pressure related to "nice girls not worrying their pretty little heads about money." And nearly always it's because they don't engage in the behaviors that will ultimately lead to wealth. Before you can become rich—and you *can* become rich—you have to know what holds you back. Let's begin with a self-assessment inventory.

NICE GIRLS DON'T GET RICH
SELF-ASSESSMENT

Consider each of the following statements and answer True if it describes you or your behavior all or most of the time and False if it rarely or never describes you or your behavior.

_____ 1. I have a concrete financial goal (an actual number) toward which I am working.

_____ 2. In the past year I have attended at least one seminar or workshop related to financial planning or investing.

_____ 3. I carry no credit card debt from month to month.

_____ 4. I balance my checkbook each month.

_____ 5. I have investments in my own name (whether you are married or partnered).

_____ 6. I take advantage of my company's perks. (If you don't know what they are, answer False.)

_____ 7. I turn down personal loan requests to people I think aren't likely to repay them.

_____ 8. I know my (or my family's) net worth.

_____ 9. I have a plan in place for how to survive financially if something catastrophic were to happen (sudden loss of a job, loss of a spouse or partner, etc.).

_____ 10. I shop on the Internet only when I have a specific purchase in mind.

_____ 11. Even if I don't prepare them, I review tax returns before signing them.

_____ 12. In addition to any retirement accounts held by my employer, I have a retirement savings account. (Answer True if you and your partner hold one in joint names.)

_____ 13. I'm comfortable asking for the salary or fee I deserve.

_____ 14. I advocate loud and clear for myself when I feel I'm not getting my fair share.

_____ 15. I'm executing a plan to live a rich life.

_____ 16. I regularly read newspapers, magazines, or articles that help me stay abreast of financial planning developments.

_____ 17. I don't feel as if I have to match the monetary value of a gift to me by giving one of similar value.

_____ 18. I know what my monthly discretionary spending budget is, and I stick to it.

_____ 19. I have taken calculated or advised risks to maximize my financial portfolio. (If you are not involved with helping to manage your family's portfolio, answer False.)

_____20. I make a profit on the products or services I provide to friends.

_____21. At the beginning of each year I plan my charitable giving.

_____22. I play the financial game to *win*.

_____23. I would have no problem requesting a prenuptial agreement that would protect my assets (or I have already done so).

_____24. I avoid shopping when I'm feeling down or blue.

_____25. I regularly analyze my spending habits.

_____26. When it comes to my money and investments, if something doesn't make sense to me, I ask probing questions.

_____27. I work in a traditionally high-paying field.

_____28. When I loan money to family or friends, I clearly state when it is due back and follow up if it's not back by that time.

_____29. I consciously explore ways to get rich other than from my current income.

_____30. Before getting married or living with someone, I had (or would have) open discussions about how we would manage money and finances.

_____31. I don't buy things priced higher than what they're worth just because it's convenient or saves me time.

_____32. I read the investment statements I receive each month. (If you don't get any, answer False.)

_____33. I make the maximum allowable contributions to my retirement plan each year.

_____34. I typically use *all* the vacation days to which I am entitled each year.

_____35. I'm a good negotiator.

_____36. I don't let people dissuade me from pursuing moneymaking plans.

_____37. My financial well-being is among my top three priorities.

_____38. I'm good at controlling the urge to buy something I want but don't need.

_____39. I meet regularly with an investment adviser (alone or with a partner) to keep a check on my financial health.

_____40. I own my own home (either alone or in joint names).

_____41. I ask my company to pay for training programs that will enhance my earning capacity.

_____42. I take full advantage of all lawful deductions on my income tax return.

SELF-ASSESSMENT SCORE SHEET

Step 1. Record your True or False responses from the questionnaire in the numbered spaces below.

Step 2. Add *down* the number of *True* responses you have in each category.

Step 3. Add your scores on the bottom line *across* for a total score.

Getting in the Money Game	Taking Charge of Your Financial Life	Spending Your Money Wisely	Learning Money Basics	Saving and Investing for Future Wealth	Maximizing Your Financial Potential at Work	Playing It Smart with Your Money	
1.	2.	3.	4.	5.	6.	7.	
8.	9.	10.	11.	12.	13.	14.	
15.	16.	17.	18.	19.	20.	21.	
22.	23.	24.	25.	26.	27.	28.	
29.	30.	31.	32.	33.	34.	35.	
36.	37.	38.	39.	40.	41.	42.	
Getting in the Money Game	Taking Charge of Your Financial Life	Spending Your Money Wisely	Learning Money Basics	Saving and Investing for Future Wealth	Maximizing Your Financial Potential at Work	Playing It Smart with Your Money	TOTAL SCORE
_____	_____	_____	_____	_____	_____	_____	_____

INTERPRETATION

Circle your two *highest* scores on the bottom line. These are the two areas in which you are most comfortable acting in ways that contribute to your financial well-being.

Circle your two *lowest* scores on the bottom line. These are the two areas in which you have the most difficulty breaking free from stereotypically feminine behaviors. Each column represents a corresponding chapter in this book. You might want to go directly to the chapters where you scored lowest, to read more about how you can address these financial development areas.

If your total score is

0–21	You'd better get moving if you ever want to lead a financially independent life. At this rate you're going to be poor or be dependent on others for the rest of your life.
22–34	You've made a good start, but you're nowhere near the finish line. Focus on those areas where you still have difficulty with becoming financially independent. You'll find that small changes pay big dividends.
35–42	If you're not already financially independent, you're doing a great job of getting there. Continue what you're doing and use this book to find some strategies for getting there even sooner.

Now, complete each of the following sentences. Don't take too much time thinking about or stewing over the statement. Whatever comes to mind initially will be as valid as something you may think of later on.

1. I'm not rich because _____.
2. And that's because _____.
3. Being rich would make me feel _____.
4. When it comes to rich people, my parents always told me _____.
5. If I focused on getting rich, it would make my partner/spouse feel _____.
6. A rich woman is one who _____.
7. What keeps me from taking more risks to get rich is _____.
8. When it comes to handling money, I _____.
9. I feel money is _____.
10. A rich woman strikes me as _____.

ANALYZING YOUR RESPONSES

Now go back and analyze each of your responses from both inventories. You may find overlapping themes or even contradictory ones. In the case of the latter, it could mean that you have gotten conflicting messages or that you disagree with the messages you received. In either case, it's not a bad thing. It's all grist for the mill. What is important is that you take time to think about your feelings and thoughts about getting rich and replace them with more realistic ones or ones that better reflect where you are now in your life. Here are some questions for you to consider:

- What are the themes that appear across my responses?
- Why do some of my responses seem contradictory?

- What are the messages playing in my head that I have to tape over if I want to be rich?
- What is the single most important thing I can do to be as rich as I would like to be?
- What current spending, saving, or investing habits do I need to *stop*?
- What current spending, saving, or investing habits do I need to *start*?
- What current spending, saving, or investing habits should I *continue* with some modifications?

The following table illuminates some of the biggest differences between how women and men deal with money. Perhaps you'll see some of your own foibles in here.

MEN, WOMEN, and MONEY

MEN	WOMEN
Invest	Save
Are socialized to learn about how to invest and make money grow	Are socialized to save money—"just in case" they have to take care of themselves
Use money to "keep score"	Use money to "take care of" others
Buy what they *need*	Buy what they *want*
Use money to prepare for the future	Use money to create a lifestyle in the present
Take investment risks	Are cautious about investing
Spend money on themselves	Spend money on those they care about
Ask for what they want	Ask for what they think they deserve
View money objectively	View money in terms of relationships
Learn how to be effective investors	Expect others to know more than they do
Gravitate toward high-paying jobs	Gravitate toward the helping professions
Advocate for themselves during trying financial times	Want to be fair during trying financial times

VISIONING YOUR FUTURE

I'm a big believer in vision. I don't see it as something magical, but rather as providing me with a focus to help me achieve my goals. When I first started my own consulting practice, after having been employed for many years by a *Fortune* 10 corporation, I was filled with fear and anxiety about my prospects for success. I could hear the voices of friends and family who were telling me it was a foolish move and one I would later regret. Then I realized it was *their* anxiety I was experiencing, not my own. I'm an intelligent woman, and I wouldn't make a decision that would in any way jeopardize my well-being. But I'm also a risk taker—something that many of the people giving me advice were not. So I adopted NASA Mission Control's famous line, "Failure is not an option," as the mantra to help support my vision. And that mantra guides my actions to this day. There may have been missteps along the way, but failure was really never an option for me. And it doesn't have to be for you either.

About ten years ago a friend of mine told me she was going to focus on being financially independent. Her mantra became, "Poor no more in '94." I can still hear her saying it. And that mantra guided all her actions. She saved enough to buy a house. She went back to school so she could get a better job. She didn't become rich in one year, but she did put herself on the path to living a more abundant life. So what's your financial vision going to be? Take a moment to think about it. Write it down. Put it in the affirmative and present tense. Some examples:

"I am acquiring all the wealth I need to live a happy and secure life."

"I am creating abundance so that I may live free of the constraints of others."
"I am rich, not only in health, friends, and family but in my
financial portfolio as well."

If you can envision it, describe it, and write it down, you
are more likely to make related decisions that will lead you to
its becoming a truth. One of my very favorite passages is from
the German philosopher Johann Goethe:

> Until one is committed, there is hesitancy,
> The chance to draw back,
> Always ineffectiveness.
> Concerning all acts of initiative and creation,
> There is one elementary truth
> The ignorance of which kills countless ideas
> And endless plans:
> That the moment one definitely commits oneself, then
> providence moves too.
> All sorts of things occur to help one that would never
> otherwise have occurred.
> A whole stream of events issues from the decision,
> Raising in one's favor all manner of unforeseen
> incidents and meetings and material assistance,
> Which no one could have dreamed would come their way.
> Whatever you can do or dream you can,
> Begin.
> Boldness has genius, power, and magic in it.
> Begin it now.

Take a moment to commit to your financial vision by writing it here:

_____

_____

_____

Write this vision on small slips of paper and put one on your bathroom mirror, in your wallet, with your checkbook, and tape one to your credit card (you'll notice that "credit card" is singular, not plural, which I will get to later). You need to see this vision before you spend money or make other financial decisions.

And while we're on the subject of envisioning your wealth, let me tell you one more story about the importance of actually visioning your future. For many years when I visited New York City for business or pleasure, I would walk by the *Today* show studio in the evening, pause, and look inside at the empty set. As I stood there, I would picture myself on the set being interviewed. I envisioned myself as comfortable and confident. So when the call came to actually appear on the show to talk about *Nice Girls Don't Get the Corner Office*, I was delighted but not exactly surprised. I had envisioned the moment just as I had envisioned having a successful business.

There are many more stories I could share with you of how positive visualization changed my life and the lives of others, but what I really want you to know is that you and you alone create your future. Dreaming it and envisioning it are part of that creation. If you aren't as rich as you want to be, my guess is that (for whatever reasons) you haven't focused on it or envisioned it as a part of your life. All I ask is that you give it a try. Turn your internal worries about money into a focus on wealth. Then follow the coaching tips in this book.

MYTHS AND MESSAGES ABOUT WOMEN AND WEALTH

The media have the power to shape our reality. From television to movies to glossy fashion magazines, a woman's self-image too often depends on what the media tell her she's *supposed* to be. Girlfriend, you have *got* to get over this hurdle if you want to be rich. If you were to be the media's ideal representation of the perfect woman, you would be thin, blond, and twenty-five. Kind of like the women on *Sex and the City*. The only stock you would own would be a "stockpile" of Manolo Blahnik shoes! Now, how many of us can say we're all that? Get real. Your ability to be rich is partially dependent on your ability to see the fallacy in the myths and messages we get about money. Here are ten myths and messages you need to exorcise:

1. It's just as easy to marry a rich man as it is a poor man. That may sound good in theory, but the fact remains that with about half of all marriages ending in divorce it's unlikely that it will help you. Marrying rich may appear to be a blessing, but it's not something you can count on. And keep in mind, there are a lot more poor men than wealthy ones.

2. You don't need to focus on getting a good education in preparation for a high-paying job, because your salary will only be a second income. A woman in one of my Nice Girl workshops said her father told her, "College is just an expensive way to find a husband." Countless women we spoke with said this was a message they received when they were growing up, and they were sorry they listened to it. In some cases it was because they married and later divorced, because they never married at all, or because they became single moms.

3. Women just aren't good with numbers—and that includes money. How many of us grew up with it being acceptable (and expected) that we wouldn't do well in math because we were girls? That myth becomes a self-fulfilling prophesy. Recent research shows that girls and boys are equally equipped to be successful in math but that girls experience more anxiety around it. One teenage girl reported, "I thought I would be considered less than feminine if I excelled in math."

4. You'll make a man feel impotent if you earn more money than he does. It's true that this phenomenon can create tension in households and on the dating scene, but it doesn't have to. Having frank discussions about money, budgets, and other financial matters can go a long way in reducing hidden feelings and resentment when it comes to a woman earning more than a man . . . or having more earning power.

5. Money can't buy you happiness. Of course, money doesn't buy happiness. And neither does poverty. It's not wealth or poverty that makes you happy or unhappy, it's how you live your life. Money simply gives you choices that you might not otherwise have. You may recall an old line from Sophie Tucker: "I've been rich and I've been poor; believe me, honey, rich is better." Of course, it's better. If you're not happy being rich, it isn't because you're rich . . . it's because you've got unresolved problems to work out. At least money *can* buy you a good therapist.

6. If you have too much money, you'll be thought of as a "rich bitch." I've certainly known rich bitches, but I've known many more poor ones. If you're a bitch *with* money, you're a bitch *without* money. There are many women who are generous in their commitment to philanthropic causes, but we don't talk about them as often as we do the more astringent ones. The term is often applied more out of jealousy than reality.

7. It's better to do good than to do well. This was the one that prevented me from accumulating wealth earlier in life. I thought it was more important to be of value to society than to get rich. I'm here to tell you, they are not mutually exclusive. You can do good *and* do well simultaneously. It's called living your values. There are many ways to make a contribution to society and get rich—and none of them include taking low-paying, female ghetto jobs. If women showed more interest in accumulating wealth, and were advocates for acquiring it, there wouldn't *be* female ghettos in the workplace.

8. It's unladylike for a woman to talk about money. Explain to me how talking about money is even remotely related to one's femininity. If you stop to think about it, it's not talking about money that bothers people, it's being *smart* that troubles them. Because knowledge and money are power and women aren't supposed to be powerful, it makes logical sense that women can't talk about money. Right? Wrong.

9. Work hard and the money will follow. This myth is true for both women and men, but women take it to the extreme. They're so busy working hard that they totally forget about getting rich. If they really thought about it, they would take some of the time they spend working hard and put that energy into managing their careers better—so they could earn more money!

10. Men are smarter than women when it comes to money. Guess what? There is no known "money gene" that men possess and women are born without. Countless stories that we heard from women involved them trusting men with their finances, only to discover the men lost, wasted, or stole their money. Remember, Columbus would never have made it to America if Queen Isabella hadn't financed the trip.

And you wonder why we have such a conflicted relationship with money? These are not messages that most men hear when growing up or as adults. These are messages we reserve for the exclusive domain of women and girls. And if you think it's any better in 2005 than it was in 1965, think again. Even though women receive strong positive messages about the importance of saving, not spending beyond their means, avoiding credit card debt, and being financially independent, they are also still faced with the myths and messages listed above. If you doubt it's true, then how would you explain the continued wage differential, differences in earned wealth, and the fact that the great majority of people who live in poverty worldwide are women and children?

HOW TO USE THIS BOOK (OR, GETTING OFF THE DIME)

Just as there isn't only one thing that prevents you from getting the corner office, there isn't just one thing that you're currently doing or not doing that is keeping you from getting rich. Some of what you read here is going to seem like common sense. You're going to say to yourself, "I already know that." Well, if you already know it, why aren't you rich? Because getting rich is about combining a mind-set with the actions you need to take to get there. That's why the following seven chapters focus not only on how you think but also on what you have to do. How you think determines how you act. So before you dismiss a particular mistake or coaching tip as "obvious," take a moment to think about why you make the mistake or why you're not engaging in the behavior suggested.

Personalize the words in this book. It's what makes this book unlike others on financial planning. It's not just a list of things to do; it's also about what you think and how you feel. You don't have to engage in every coaching tip suggested in this book to get rich. If you commit to doing just one-tenth of them, you will be well on the path to taking control of your financial future.

Chapters 2 to 8 describe key elements essential for financial success. Each corresponds directly with one of the columns on the Nice Girls Don't Get Rich Self-Assessment. I suggest that you go first to the sections that most closely correlate with your *lowest* responses on the assessment. This is where you will find the most help related to understanding your unique reasons for avoiding financial independence and tips for how to change those behaviors. Once you're done reading these sections, don't tell yourself you're going to do everything suggested in the coaching tips. That would set you up to fail. Instead, as you go along, check the coaching suggestions to which you can commit and take the time to write these behaviors on the Action Plan contained at the very end of the book.

As Goethe said, "the moment one definitely commits oneself, then providence moves too." The universe rewards action. You will find that when you commit to being financially independent—however you define it—you will look differently at the world, your relationship with money, and the behaviors that contribute to (or hinder you from) getting rich. "Nice girls" don't get rich because they focus more on the needs of others than on their own needs and avoid taking the steps required to become truly independent. You won't get rich by being a "nice girl," but you can by becoming an adult woman—and don't let anyone tell you otherwise.

Chapter Two

Getting in the Money Game

*There is always an inner game being played in your mind
no matter what outer game you are playing. How aware
you are of this game can make the difference between
success and failure in the outer game.*

TIM GALLWEY

In *Nice Girls Don't Get the Corner Office* I talked about the
workplace being a game, with the corner office being a
metaphor for achieving your professional goals. Getting rich
is also a game. It has rules, strategies, an end point, and a language all its own. Too many women fail to achieve their
financial goals because they don't play the game. You may
have played the game of Monopoly when you were younger.
Do you remember competing to buy those properties, rail-
roads, and utilities? Even though you were earning only play
money, you probably played the game to win. When did you
lose this sense of competition in relation to money?

All these years later, the one thing I distinctly remember
about playing Monopoly with my brothers and cousins is that
the girls rarely won. No matter how hard we tried, the boys
seemed to trump us. They were more competitive, strategic,

and focused on the end goal. They were also less likely to "play nice," as our mothers instructed. As early as childhood, women begin to have difficulty with competing successfully to accumulate money. In order to achieve their financial goals, women need to get this drive back. We must *play to win*.

In sports psychology there's something called the inner game, a term coined by Tim Gallwey. He says that performance equals potential minus interference. For women, getting rich is fraught with interference in the form of self-limiting inner messages, social messages, and the very real challenges of getting our fair share in a world that often sees us more as helpmates, nurturers, and accommodators than equal players. One of the ways you overcome interference is by visualizing and preparing for success. Use this chapter to help you get onto the playing field and play to win. And if you haven't played Monopoly in a while, I suggest you go back and play it one more time. Use it as a warm-up for getting to the *real* game of money. Maybe I would have won more Monopoly games had I known about the inner game back then.

Mistake 1

Striving for Survival, Not Wealth

*M*any women are justifiably proud for having survived on their earnings, but they haven't really focused on how to thrive. They may have what they *need* but not what they *want*. Messages such as "Don't be greedy" or "Learn to be happy with what you have" are forms of interference that preclude you from looking beyond the present to a financially rewarding future. Accumulating wealth—no matter how much—requires first having a crystal clear mind's-eye picture of being surrounded with money.

Allison is an example of a woman who moved from living what she described as a minimalist life to one of fulfillment. Three years ago she was earning an annual salary of $60,000 at her job as a social worker, contributed about $8,000 a year to her agency's retirement plan, and was content but not satisfied. She had everything she needed, but not what she most wanted: to travel the world. When she and I first met more than five years ago, she talked about her dreams as if they were just that: dreams. Nothing she ever really hoped to attain. I suggested that she start visioning what she would like her life to look like—without limitations. At first it was hard for her to get beyond the inner voice that told her she couldn't possibly do what she wanted and still survive, but she kept working at it. She pictured herself with a private practice of psychotherapy, enough money and time to travel to places she'd always wanted to see, and the opportunity to explore a more spiritual life. She spent time speaking with women who had successfully transitioned from surviving to thriving, and she learned from their stories.

With each passing month Allison had not only a clearer

vision of what she wanted but also an idea of what it would take to achieve it. She began saving money so that she could leave her job and have enough to pay for her basic necessities. Within three years of considering the fact that she could live her life differently, she was. She did resign from her agency, found shared office space, and hung her therapist's shingle. Today she has a thriving practice, put $30,000 into savings and other investments last year, works four days a week, keeps Fridays open as her "spirit" day, and has traveled throughout France and England. And it all began with a laser-focused vision. In the first chapter you wrote a brief financial vision statement. Now it's time to consider how you can achieve it.

COACHING TIPS

- **Envision your life as you want it to be, not as it is.** This isn't as easy as it sounds. Picturing your life differently requires getting beyond the mental interference that inevitably arises. That interference isn't necessarily a bad thing. In fact, it prevents you from taking foolish risks and causes you to consider potential stumbling blocks. Each night before you go to sleep let your mind wander to an image of how you would like to live your life, free from financial constraints. What are you doing? Whom are you doing it with? What does it feel like?

- **Talk to people who took risks to achieve their d.eams.** Their stories and experiences can help you to gain insight into what it takes to overcome the fears and obstacles associated with change.

- **Share your vision with trusted friends.** Once you gain clarity about what you want to do, say it out loud. Talk about what you're thinking and ask for their support. Putting words to your vision begins the process of moving it from a dream to reality.

Mistake 2

Not Creating a Financial Goal

"Would you tell me, please, which way I ought to go
from here?" asked Alice.
"That depends a good deal on where you want to get to,"
said the Cat.
"I don't much care where," said Alice.
"Then it doesn't matter which way you go," said the
Cat.
"So long as I get somewhere," Alice added as an
explanation.
"Oh, you're sure to do that," said the Cat, "if you only
walk long enough."

LEWIS CARROLL,
Alice in Wonderland

If you don't have a financial goal, you'll be walking for a long time. How much do you need in order to live your life free from concerns about money? What's the dollar figure? Are you currently running the financial race with no finish line in sight? Why would you go to work every day without an idea of how much money you need to live the life you want? Are you accumulating *things* in lieu of accumulating *wealth*? If you don't have a financial goal in mind, you're only running in place.

In training programs I often ask if there are any runners in the group. Inevitably, a few hands go up. I then ask those people if they start their runs with the idea in mind that they will go out, start running, and run until they drop. They typically laugh and say of course not. They have an idea not only of how long their run will take but also of the path they will follow along the way. The same holds true for tennis players, golfers, and other athletes. They envision their swings, placing the ball where they want, and imagine winning the point. Accumulating wealth is no different. You've got to know where you're going and have a plan to get there if you want to win this game.

Use the chart on the next page to get started. At the bottom write down how much you have in savings today. At the top write down what your financial goal is. This can be a short-term or long-term goal. For instance, you might want to save for a down payment on a car or home. Or you might want to accumulate a particular dollar figure that will allow you to retire by age fifty. Every so often fill in how much closer you are toward your goal. There will be hurdles to over-come as well, such as when you've saved $1,000 to put into your retirement account and then your car breaks down. Or you finally reached an annual financial goal and you have to withdraw money to pay for roof repairs. Don't let these finan-cial challenges discourage you, though—it's a marathon, not a sprint. Take it one step at a time.

COACHING TIPS

• **Calculate your financial goal.** This isn't a number you pull out of thin air. *Current savings + amount needed to achieve your vision = your financial goal.* It may be that you want to purchase your own home. Or be able to take a trip to an exotic place each year. You may want to retire in the next five years. Your goal may be modest or aggressive. It may also change as you get closer to achieving it. The important thing is to know how much money you need and to not be afraid to step on the financial scale.

• **Start researching.** Putting together the actual financial requirement to achieve your vision is an empowering exercise. It puts you one step closer to making your vision a reality. If you want to own your home, go to a bank or mortgage lender and find out what you can afford. If you want to start your own business, learn about how much it will cost. As Confucius said, "The journey of a thousand miles begins with a single step."

REACHING YOUR FINANCIAL FINISH LINE

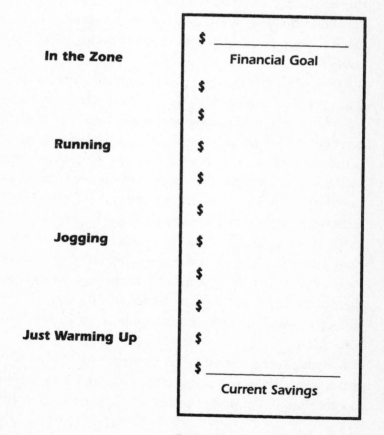

In the Zone

$ _____

Financial Goal

$

$

Running

$

$

$

Jogging

$

$

$

Just Warming Up

$

$ _____

Current Savings

Mistake 3

Not Knowing Your Net Worth

*A*pplying for a mortgage? Writing a will? Seeking financial aid for college? Or just looking to build your wealth? No matter what your financial circumstances or goals, you can't plan for tomorrow until you know where you stand today," says Allen Jones, senior vice president and director of the Merrill Lynch Private Client Marketing Group. Consider yourself a business—you are, after all, in the business of getting rich, aren't you? And you wouldn't run a business without knowing what your assets are, how much is coming in, how much is going out, and how to build the profitability of that business.

Many women don't want to know their net assets any more than they want to know their weight. If you won't step on the scale because you don't want to know, then you probably don't know your net worth either. Simply put, your net worth is the total value of your assets (savings, retirement funds, home, car, etc.) less your liabilities (outstanding loans, credit card debt, etc.). Knowing your net worth doesn't have to be depressing. Studies conducted by Jay Zagorsky, a research scientist at the Center for Human Resource Research at Ohio State University and Boston University School of Management, suggest that 70 percent of households underestimate their net worth and 25 percent overestimate their wealth. Those who underestimate their wealth do so by nearly 40 percent!

Knowing your net worth helps you to live your life as richly as you want. Whereas a budget helps you with the month-to-month picture, knowing your net worth provides you with insight into the bigger picture. It tells you whether you can afford to contribute to your favorite charity or buy the home of your dreams.

COACHING TIPS

• **Calculate your net worth.** There are a number of ways you can do this. On the following page is a work sheet that will help you get started. And if you go to www.young money.com/calculators, under Personal Finance you'll find a net worth calculator. I like this particular one because it also projects what your net worth might be if your portfolio continued to grow at a fixed rate. Take a few minutes to determine where you are now . . . and where you want to be five years from now.

• **Calculate the amount of money you need to live comfortably in retirement.** Go to the Internet, do a search for "retirement calculator," and pay a visit to one of the many sites that perform this service for you free of charge. It is a little like stepping on that scale. You don't always want to know what it will read, but it's better to know so that you can do something about it than to pretend it's not important to your health. Knowing how much you will need in retirement is a big part of your wealth health.

ASSETS (What you own)
Use Current Market Values

CASH AND SAVINGS
Cash and checking accounts _____
Savings accounts _____
Certificates of deposit _____
Money market instruments _____
Other _____

Total $ _____

INVESTMENT ASSETS
Stocks _____
Bonds _____
Mutual funds _____
Employee stock options _____
Cash value of life insurance _____
Surrender value of annuities _____
Income-producing real estate _____
Other _____

Total $ _____

RETIREMENT ASSETS
Pension or profit-sharing plans _____
IRAs, Keogh accounts _____
Employee savings plans, 401(k)s _____
Other _____

Total $ _____

NON-INCOME-EARNING ASSETS
Home _____
Non-income real estate _____
Furniture and equipment _____
Autos _____
Recreational vehicle, boat, etc. _____
Collectibles _____
Jewelry _____
Other _____

Total $ _____

TOTAL ASSETS $ _____

Courtesy Wimmerassociates com

WORK SHEET

LIABILITIES (What you owe)
Use Current Outstanding Balances

Home mortgage   _____
Other mortgages or notes   _____
Installment debts   _____
Credit cards and charge accounts   _____
Other loans   _____
Taxes not withheld   _____
Current unpaid bills   _____
Amount borrowed on life insurance   _____
Other   _____

TOTAL LIABILITIES $ _____

TOTAL ASSETS $ _____
TOTAL LIABILITIES   (subtract) $ _____

NET WORTH $ _____
(Assets minus liabilities)

Mistake 4

Not Playing to Win

$\mathscr{I}$f you're not accumulating the amount of money you need to be financially independent, ask yourself why. Are you better at playing the role of "nice girl" than you are at playing the financial game? You don't need an abundance of testosterone to be competitive, but you do need a burning in your belly to live the life you *want*, not the life you *have*. One reason why men are more likely to be wealthy than women is that they know what it means to play the game to win.

I sometimes play golf with children. Even in a game like golf where you're really playing against yourself and the course, boys play far more competitively than girls. The boys will consistently shave points off their scores by taking mulligans (a free second shot following a shot that was played poorly). The girls count each and every stroke to the point where they become discouraged with having such high scores. When I say something to the boys about their scores not being an accurate reflection of how they played the game, they typically shrug it off with, "It's just a game."

Men bring this same willingness to win at all costs to their financial lives. It's gotten more than a few men into trouble (think Enron, WorldCom, etc.), but generally speaking, playing the game to win means you are more likely to walk away with more than you would if you simply played like a girl—fair to a fault, polite, and more concerned with how others perceive you than with winning. One of the basic precepts of negotiating is that those who ask for more going in walk out with more. And there's nothing illegal or unethical about expecting to walk away a winner.

COACHING TIPS

• **Play a competitive sport or game.** It doesn't matter if it's bridge, tennis, or chess. The point is to get in the habit of playing to win. Games and sports give you the opportunity to learn about strategy and competition. You can learn every bit as much from a Scrabble tournament as you can from a golf tournament.

• **Think twice about your definition of "fair."** Women and men define the word far differently. Whereas men consider it anything short of illegal, women tend to consider it in relation to how a decision or action will impact another person. Both are right, but they're not mutually exclusive. You can play to win *and* be concerned with people. It just takes tuning out that voice in the back of your head that tells you it's impossible to do both.

• **Keep your eye on the finish line.** When you overlook what it is you most want—to win—you let go of the strategies needed to get there. When it comes to your financial finish, post your goal where you'll see it every single day. Whether it's an actual dollar figure, a home, or a lifestyle, create a visual of it and put it on your bathroom mirror, your refrigerator, and inside your top desk drawer. That's your finish line.

Mistake 5

Listening to Naysayers

*W*hen I left a good-paying job at a prestigious company to start my own business in 1986, there wasn't a person in my network who had anything good to say about my decision. My mother told me just the thought of my being "unemployed" made her "stomach churn." My best friend told me it made her "nervous." So not only did I have to deal with my own feelings of anxiety over my decision, I had to deal with theirs too. Contrast this with my brothers, who started their own businesses after working for big firms. They didn't get the same negative messages. Whether it's because people don't think a woman can be as successful in business as a man, or because they simply believe a woman should spend her time caring for others, the result is the same. Many women remain in unfulfilling, low-paying jobs because they listen to people who don't support their vision of future possibilities.

A 2001 U.S. Census Bureau report reveals there are 5.4 million women-owned businesses in the United States, they employ 7.1 million people, and, in 1997, they generated $818.7 billion in receipts. That's a lot of women making a lot of money and putting a lot of beans on the family table. In the past decade there has been a steady increase in the number of women who start their own businesses. But this isn't to say that you have to start your own business to get rich.

One young woman told me that her CPA father always instilled in her the need to save, but not necessarily invest. As a result, she keeps her money in a savings account where, for the past few years, it has earned less than 2 percent annually. Another woman reported that she stayed in a low-paying job because her husband convinced her she couldn't possibly do better elsewhere. And yet another woman to whom I spoke revealed that she doesn't charge for the items she knits for family and friends because her parents taught her that money and friendship shouldn't be mixed.

There will always be naysayers in your life. Some truly have your best interests at heart, but others may be jealous or small-minded. Although you want the input of people who may be able to help you avoid the pitfalls on your path to wealth, you don't want them to determine the direction of that path.

COACHING TIPS

• **Use your research as an offensive tactic.** You can head naysayers off at the pass if you have data to support your intended direction. The data will also make you more confident so that you're less inclined to listen to them in the first place.

• **Be clear about what you want when you ask for opinions . . . or don't ask at all!** Rather than asking friends or family members whether they think something you're about to do is a good idea, ask them about their experiences related to the direction. For example, "I'm considering investing in a real estate investment trust. Have you ever made a similar investment and, if so, what have your results been?" This prevents uneducated, inexperienced people from dumping their unfounded opinions on you.

• **Surround yourself with yeasayers.** Identify the most positive and upbeat, yet realistic and practical, people in your life and make them your "advisory board." Every woman needs a cheering squad (men already have them—they're called moms and wives). Ask these people if you can use them as sounding boards.

- **Don't throw the baby out with the bathwater.** There are times when a naysayer actually has something valuable to add to your decision-making process. So don't entirely dismiss naysayers' input—just take it with a pound (not just a grain) of salt.

Mistake 6

Setting Artificial Boundaries

*F*uturist Joel Barker says that paradigms are a good thing because they help us order the world. But they're a bad thing, he adds, when they limit us from being able to see what's on the periphery. A woman's paradigm of what she can and can't be is often much narrower than a man's. As I said earlier, even if you get all the right messages from your parents about having limitless opportunities, the world doesn't always validate those notions. As a result, we may unknowingly choose to live within artificially narrowed boundaries.

Whether you feel as if you're stuck in a low-paying field or sick of having a $3,000 monthly mortgage which prevents you from doing the thing you would most love to do, chances are it's because you're stuck in your life paradigm. *It's just how things are,* you think to yourself. Well, things don't just have to be that way. How you live your life is a choice, not a prison sentence. And in life you don't get credit for time served.

Remember, being rich isn't only about having accumulated financial wealth, *it's about having the amount of money you need to live your life the way you want free from concerns about money.* If you're earning a terrific living but not living the life you want, you're no richer than the woman living in poverty trying to climb out of her financial hole. You both have difficult choices to make and risks to take. I see it all the time. I can be coaching a woman executive earning upwards of $300,000 annually, but she's not happy. She's become so accustomed to that income that she really can't see that she could choose to live differently. She could sell her Manhattan town house, get rid of the Mercedes, *and* live her dreams—if only she reevaluated her priorities.

Such self-imposed false dichotomies can also work in reverse. You may be living your values but not earning enough to live the life you really want. Could it be that you're stuck in some old paradigm based on the notion that money won't make you happy? Whether you are living your values but not living the kind of abundant life you would like, or living an abundant life but not living your values, you are enjoying only a portion of life as opposed to life to the fullest. Money per se does not make you happy—it's what it enables you to do with your life. Too many women live trapped in the paradoxical paradigm of "money can't make me happy" or "more money will make me happier." Both are true, but again, they're not mutually exclusive. The ability to simultaneously hold two disparate beliefs and reconcile them in some manner is what it takes to become rich.

COACHING TIPS

• **Take stock of *your* values (as well as valuing your stock).** Notice the emphasis on the word *your*. It's not what Mom, Dad, or society tells you should be valued, it's what *you* value. Valuing money is no better or worse than valuing making a contribution to your community. Just make sure that you're clear about whose life you're living—your own or the one others think you should be living. Try taking this little test. Circle the three, four, or five value statements that most closely reflect your values. If something that you value isn't on the list, add it.

1. Spiritual fulfillment
2. Health

3. Family and/or friends
4. Helping people
5. Financial security
6. Making a difference in society
7. Affiliation with groups or people who share my values
8. Recognition—being known as an "expert" in my field
9. Influence
10. Creativity—writing, drawing, building, designing, etc.
11. Knowledge—learning about new ideas and things
12. Having stability in my life
13. Variety—not being stuck doing just one thing
14. Aesthetics—being surrounded by or pursuing beautiful places or things
15. Money—whether or not it allows me to live my values
16. Excitement
17. Independence—not being told what to do
18. Physical challenges
19. Time—not being constrained by what I'm supposed to do
20. Travel

Now think about the life you're currently living. Are your values a significant thread in the fabric of your life? If not, it's time to start making the changes—perhaps difficult changes—that will make them so. Align your life with your values—and find a way to prosper at the same time!

• **Read** *Feel the Fear—and Do It Anyway.* This book by Susan Jeffers (Ballantine, 1988) urges you to acknowledge the fears that hold you back from achieving your life goals or overcoming obstacles, but also to train yourself to overcome those fears through positive thinking, goal setting, and assertive behaviors. You may be afraid to sell your house and move to that small town you've been wanting to live in, but this doesn't mean you can't do it. It only means you have to prioritize your values and create a plan for how you can realistically do it. One of my favorite quotes is from Eleanor Roosevelt: "You gain courage and confidence from doing the things you think you cannot do."

Mistake 7

Not Balancing the Strategic with the Tactical

*I*n my book *Overcoming Your Strengths: 8 Reasons Why Successful People Derail and How to Remain on Track*, I talk about the importance of not only being able to envision the big or long-term picture but also being able to develop the tactics required to achieve it. Although in that book I was referring to business projects, the same holds true when it comes to getting—and staying—in the financial game. Your life strategy may be to retire at age fifty with $1 million in the bank, but your tactics are all the actions you are required to take in the meantime to get you there.

Most people are born with the inclination to focus on either details or the big picture. It's what makes some people go into jobs at the Internal Revenue Service, while others gravitate to places like NASA or the Jet Propulsion Laboratory. Long-term success is dependent on being able to hold the long-term goal in mind while taking all the actions needed to make it a reality. Too many people rely on one or the other, thereby missing out on obvious opportunities.

The late Mary Kay Ash, founder of Mary Kay Cosmetics, displayed the unique ability to blend the strategic with the tactical, and it made her a multimillionaire. She started with a vision for creating a cosmetics company that enabled women to become financially independent and where God could come first, family second, and work third in their lives. Then she systematically went about getting the funding, hiring the right people, and developing the processes needed to turn her vision into reality. Keep this in mind: *A vision without a plan is a dream, and a plan without vision is marching in place.*

COACHING TIPS

• **Brainstorm your financial game plan with big-picture thinkers.** Who are the people in your life who always seem to come up with the most creative, out-of-the-box ideas? You may dismiss them as "dreamers," but they're exactly the people you need to help you think outside of whatever financial box you're currently in. Invite them over to your home for a brainstorming session where you share your vision with them, and ask them for ideas about achieving it. Resist the temptation to throw out far-fetched ideas—when you later think about them, they just could work.

• **Get advice from nitpickers.** You know, those people who get so involved in the details that they sometimes suffer from analysis paralysis. They provide the perfect counterpoint to the dreamers. Ask them for help with developing an actual game plan for the steps you need to take to achieve your financial vision. In this case avoid the inclination to get bored with the details—that's precisely what you need to develop a firm foundation on which to run your financial race.

Mistake 8

Staying in Your Safety Zone

*S*ometimes the most obvious mistakes are right in front of you and you don't see them. After my colleague Dr. Kim Finger read a first draft of this manuscript, she reminded me that the risks I took in starting my own business seventeen years ago contributed to accumulating my own wealth. She suggested I share with you my own story about how I transitioned from being an employee to becoming an employer. In effect, I changed my game entirely, and that was the turning point in my life—personally, professionally, and financially.

As I mentioned earlier, I worked for a large corporation but wasn't really happy. The company paid for me to complete my doctoral education, and once I had that degree in my hand, I asked if I could be transferred to a department where I could use it. Fortunately for me, jobs in that department were few and turnover was low, which meant I would have to wait a long time if I ever wanted to use my doctorate in counseling psychology within the company. Being the impatient sort, I began planning how I could leave and start my own business.

At the time, I wasn't unlike the many other people who live comfortably as long as they're employed (the working rich). I had retirement savings and not much more. When the company went through a period of downsizing and was offering separation packages, I jumped at the chance. I was told I wasn't eligible to receive the package because I wasn't someone they wanted to let go. So I negotiated. If I would agree to stay one more year, they would give me the package. That extra year was a blessing in disguise. I used the time to start saving, prepare my business plan, and prepare psychologically for leaving a good job with good benefits and stature in the community. As if it were yesterday, I can recall the feeling of walking out of the building on my last day of work. I was scared and apprehensive about what the future held for me. But I used that fear to propel me into action.

I started off by opening a psychotherapy practice in downtown Los Angeles. I knew there were people who would want to come for counseling during the workday, and, at the time, there weren't many therapists practicing in the downtown area. I would be lying if I said there weren't some lean times. After the first year, with only the amount of money needed to cover one more month's expenses, I took out a home equity line of credit against my home. But over and over I told myself, "Failure is not an option." It became my mantra and helped me envision success. More important, I never doubted my decision to work for myself—I simply wanted to be successful.

Before long, I was getting calls from colleagues around the country who knew I did training in my previous job, asking if I could do workshops for their companies. It wasn't what I had planned (especially after studying for five years at night to become a therapist), but I was willing to explore the possibilities. Then came the call that changed my professional life. It was from a good client and now dear friend, Dr. Karen Otazo, who asked me to coach one of her employees. Remember, this was more than fifteen years ago and business coaching was not the trend it is today. I told her I didn't know what that was, and she explained it would be like a one-on-one training program. With my background in business, training, and psychotherapy, she thought I would be a natural.

Starting with that first client, I developed a unique model for business coaching. Within a year from the time Karen called me, I made the shift from being a psychotherapist to being an executive coach—a lucrative and personally rewarding profession. Within five years from the time I walked away from my job, I had a successful consulting practice that enabled me to live the life I wanted, free from concerns about money. In other words, I was rich. And now, seventeen years later, I do only the kinds of work I most love to do, choose the clients with whom I want to work, and have the opportunity to travel the world—on someone else's dime. To this day I keep the same sign in my office that I had when I started my business, to serve as a reminder that taking risks pays off: NO GUTS, NO GLORY.

COACHING TIPS

• **Dare to dream.** It may sound cliché, but too many people stay in unsatisfying or low-paying jobs because they don't dare to dream about what would make them happy. I know, because I was one of those people. Both of my parents worked in traditional jobs—and worked hard—to support their family. But it seemed as if they worked for the day they could retire. I thought that was how life was supposed to be and resigned myself to working for someone else for the rest of my life. Then I started dreaming about what I would love to do, and those dreams caused me to take all the steps needed to make them a reality. It's that vision thing again.

• **Manage your lifestyle.** In the beginning, starting your own business requires taking stock of what's really important to you and letting go of the material things that you've come to rely on for satisfaction. You might not be able to quit your job and still make your annual pilgrimage to Tuscany. The new BMW every two years might be out of the question initially. But so what? What would you be willing to trade for the chance of having the life you now only dream of?

• **Consider a small-business loan.** There's money available to entrepreneurs with a good credit history and great ideas. The U.S. Small Business Administration provides a wealth of information and technical assistance about getting a business started. There's even an entire section for women entrepreneurs. Go to their Web site at www.sbaonline.sba.gov and learn more about whether you have what it takes to start your own business and the kind of help they can provide if you do.

• **Talk to your significant other or trusted friends about your dream.** When I coach executives who are unhappy in their jobs and want to do something different, they often feel they won't get the support they need from those around them. I encourage them to talk about what they really want with the people in their lives who matter most. They are often surprised to find that others are willing to make the changes and sacrifices needed to help them get started.

Chapter Three

Taking Charge of Your Financial Life

As soon as many women think of incurring someone else's displeasure—especially a man's—they equate it with abandonment. If women avoid taking this risk, in most cases they cannot begin the journey.

JEAN BAKER MILLER,
Towards a New Psychology of Women

Although *all* the mistakes in this book relate to acting like a girl, this chapter examines those behaviors that relate most directly to the childhood messages we get and how they influence our relationship with money. As I mentioned earlier, women get mixed messages in childhood: *You can do anything you want . . . but it wouldn't hurt to find someone who will take good care of you.* As a result, we are achieving more in business, education, and other fields, but that's not translating into accumulated wealth. Getting rich requires that you be at the helm (or at least be a cocaptain) of your financial ship—and I don't mean the ship of fools. To do this, you've got to be smart about money, involved with how your money is spent and invested, and get a financial life.

Even among the women we surveyed and spoke with who indicated they were told by parents to be financially independent (which seems more common among younger women), there is still a double bind. Regardless of what they hear from their parents, they enter into a world where they are made to feel that men know more when it comes to money, that women are responsible for the household, and that if it comes to a choice between taking care of themselves or others—well, it's not really a choice, after all. As a result, women wind up acting in ways more consistent with the messages the culture gives them related to money than with the messages they receive from their families—or even with their own instincts. They fall victim to subtle social messages that imply it's better to feign ignorance, acquiesce to a man's purported financial acumen, and not risk damaging a man's ego by becoming too closely involved with money matters. Following the tips in this chapter will help you gain the knowledge and confidence needed to take charge of your financial life.

Mistake 9

Not Making Your Financial Well-Being a Priority

*W*omen treat their financial lives a little like they treat their cars. Until that red warning light goes on that shouts *Low on oil*, we don't make the time to protect this valuable asset. We may not *have* the time, but we *make* the time to pick up the laundry, do the grocery shopping, and buy birthday or holiday gifts for friends and family. And why? Because these are things we often do for *other* people, not just for ourselves. A woman's mind-set is all too often about doing for others at the expense of taking care of our own needs. It's all part of the "nice girl" syndrome.

When asked what prevented her from acquiring the wealth she needed to live a financially independent life, one woman told us this:

> The most stupid thing I've done around money is to think that devoting time to finances and financial goals should come second to working hard and building a career. I can see that whenever I am too busy, I let fifty dollars here or twenty dollars there slip through my fingers. Or worse, I missed the opportunity to refinance a home loan when rates were so low because I didn't make time to look into it. We forget that these small errors compound into a very big difference in achieving financial goals.

Making your financial well-being a priority means several things: taking time to learn about finances, taking time to invest, and taking time to track your portfolio. When it's not something that particularly interests you or something that you feel proficient at, it becomes even easier to avoid it altogether. If you want to be able to live a life free from the burden of worrying about money, your financial well-being must become just as important as those little things you do for everyone else that eat up so much of your time. It's not about totally ignoring the niceties, it's about losing the guilt associated with doing something *just for you*.

If you stop to think about it, it's not only planning your financial future that takes a backseat to the needs of others. It can be postponing a doctor's appointment because you can't find the time, not getting to the gym because someone at work needs something from you, or canceling that appointment for a massage because someone else's needs seem more important at the moment. Being more concerned about the needs of others than about their own needs often precludes women from making time for themselves—and that includes making time to create a solid financial future.

COACHING TIPS

• **Schedule "get rich" time.** If you're reading this, then you've already invested time and money in your financial well-being. Good work! Now take your calendar or PDA and block out one hour per month as time you'll use to start getting rich. I mean *now*. Get up, get your calendar, and enter it as a recurring event. You can use that time to read a magazine on investing, do Internet research, or talk to your spouse or a family member about financial matters. Make the time sacrosanct—nothing short of a bona fide emergency should cause you to cancel it.

- **Be conscious of how you spend your time.** Your time is exactly like money. Once it's spent, there's no retrieving it. Make certain you're investing it wisely. If you're not living your life consciously in other ways, you certainly won't be conscious about how you spend and invest money. Before simply agreeing or offering to do something for someone else, consider what it will cost you and if that's a price you're willing to pay. Remember, doing for others is often nothing more than a legitimate way to avoid what you know you should be doing for yourself.

- **Give yourself permission to be selfish.** At least that's what it feels like when you take time out for yourself—selfish. So be it. Call it what you like, but when it comes right down to it, no one can take better care of you than yourself. And there's nothing wrong with taking care of yourself. Too many women have been socialized to believe it's a mortal sin to spend time on themselves. Whether it's taking care of your financial, physical, or emotional needs, allow yourself to be indulgent for some portion of each day, week, and month. Sometimes you just need to be selfish to be self-sufficient.

Mistake 10

Choosing to Remain Financially Illiterate

$\mathscr{B}$arbara Stanny, in her book *Prince Charming Isn't Coming: How Women Get Smart About Money* (Putnam Penguin, 1997), tells the story of how at twenty-one years old she inherited millions of dollars from her father, Richard Block of the well-known tax preparation firm H&R Block. When she married, she turned it over to her husband to manage. Her husband was not only a certified financial planner, he was a compulsive gambler. Within ten years of being married, he managed to completely lose her fortune.

After appearing together on a CNN special about women and money, Barbara and I spoke by phone one Sunday afternoon. The burning question in my mind was how an intelligent, educated woman could allow this to happen. Here's what she told me:

> Unconscious messages were in control of me. I found money so scary and intimidating—my brain would fog and my eyes would glaze over. Even when 1 knew he was gambling, I didn't want it to be true. I wanted to believe the myth that I would somehow be taken care of. One day I even went to a financial coach to help me take control, but when I left his office, I felt I was doing something wrong. I thought men were supposed to take care of the money and women were supposed to take care of the men. I never went back to the coach because I felt so strongly I had done a bad thing. It wasn't until after my money was lost and I was in therapy that I realized my deepest fear was that if I was smart about money, I would never find a man to love me.

Being financially illiterate is a choice, just as the decision to get rich is a choice. My personalized license plate says CHOISEZ because I believe all is chosen. In addition to Barbara's comment that money and finances can be so intimidating as to leave you fearful about learning about them, the women I spoke with revealed several other reasons for remaining financially illiterate: (1) They don't have the time to learn about investing or to focus on their finances, (2) they're not interested in financial matters, or (3) they learned from Mom that "dumbing down" about money would make them more attractive to men (one woman described herself as a "recovering dumb blonde"). Whatever the reason, you can allow others to have control of your financial future, or you can choose to take the time to learn about how to be in charge of your own wealth. The chart on the next page shows just how many women don't take the time to develop their financial knowledge.

Similarly, I know there are many things you're not interested in but you do them, because they in some way contribute to your well-being. I often think of the discipline it takes to get rich as being similar to the discipline it takes to lose weight. In fact, one woman I spoke with, a financial planner in Anchorage, Alaska, told me she noticed a correlation between a woman's financial life and her weight. The more out of control her eating, the more out of control her spending. (She was honest about the fact that she hasn't scientifically validated her observations.)

Becoming financially literate requires discipline. You may not do it because you *want* to—there are many things more fun that you could think of—you do it because it's good for you. You do it because it will help you achieve your personal goals. You do it because the thought of being financially independent far outweighs the thought of living a life controlled by others.

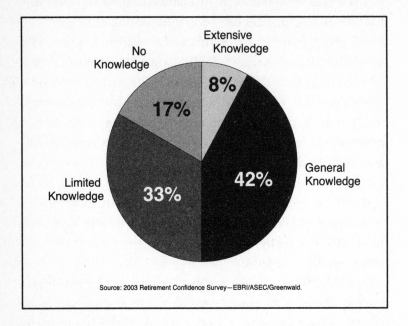

No Knowledge

Extensive Knowledge

8%

17%

General Knowledge

Limited Knowledge

33%

42%

Source: 2003 Retirement Confidence Survey—EBRI/ASEC/Greenwald.

COACHING TIPS

Based on her own experience and learning the hard way, here are three great suggestions from Barbara Stanny on beginning to improve your financial literacy:

• **Give yourself three to six months without *doing* anything.** Instead, spend some portion of *every day* reading something about money—even if it's just the headlines of the business section of the paper. So much about being smarter about money is just familiarizing yourself with it. Says Stanny, "I put section C of the *Wall Street Journal* on the kitchen counter every morning for months before I finally stopped to read it. Turn on CNBC, read magazines, and get in the habit of inundating yourself with the information."

• **Talk about money.** In our society we don't talk about money. *Every week* have a conversation about money—preferably with someone who knows more about it than you. Ask how people manage their money. Pick their brains. Form a study group and together talk about books and articles related to money. Talk about the personal issues you're having around money. Don't be afraid to go into therapy, if you think it's necessary, to find out about your own mental blocks when it comes to becoming financially independent.

• **Start saving.** It doesn't matter if it's $5 or $500. Get in the savings habit. *Every month* automatically transfer a set amount from your checking account to your savings account and retirement fund. If you have an emergency, you will now have a place to go other than your parents, friends, or, worse yet, ex-husband. After a few months, start investing in mutual funds that you've been reading and talking about. Before long, you will realize that *compounding* is, as Ben Franklin said, "a thing of beauty."

And here are a few more tips from me to help you get into the money game:

• **Commit to attending one financial investment seminar within the next three months.** This isn't a major investment of time. You can find these classes at community colleges, extension programs, credit unions, and even online. Many investment firms offer short evening programs designed for the financial novice. They're often advertised in the business section of the Sunday paper. If you don't see one offered, call your local American Express Financial Services office, Merrill Lynch, or TD Waterhouse and ask when their next program will be. A word of caution: *Resist any sales pitches*. Don't feel as if you have to buy something or open an account with the firm just because you went to the seminar. If pressured, simply say, "I came here tonight to learn more and I'd like to think about it now."

• **Subscribe to (and read) a financial planning magazine.** There are plenty to choose from, including *Money*, *Smart-Money*, *Kiplinger's Personal Finance*, and *Worth*. Don't allow these to collect dust on the coffee table—use a portion of your scheduled "get rich" time to actually read them, although you needn't feel as if you have to read the entire magazine. Instead, read just one article that you think might interest you. It's all part of easing your way into the world of investing.

• **Put a link to www.moneycentral.msn.com on your desktop.** If you look beyond all of the advertising, you'll find it a valuable resource in terms of articles, ideas, and strategies. When you finish up one project and before you start the next, take a break by pulling up and perusing the site.

• **Scan the front page of the Money section of *USA Today*.** The articles are concise and written in lay terms. If you invest only ten to fifteen minutes per day (use it as an excuse to take a break), you'll soon become familiar with trends, companies, types of investments, and other financial topics.

• **Use commuting time as learning time.** Listen to radio programs that focus on business and finance. The call-in questions will help you to see you're not alone.

Mistake 11

Being a Financial Ostrich

*B*eing left financially unprepared is one thing. Being financially incapable of managing what you're left with is another. Plenty of women find themselves suddenly faced with having to take control of the financial reins because of divorce or their partner's death or incapacitation. Some women are lucky enough to be left in great financial shape where they don't have to worry about money, just about managing it. But others are faced with having to do some belt-tightening or financial planning. In either case the question to ask yourself is, "Do I know enough about our family finances to be able to step in and take over?" If the answer is no, you've gotta get out of the backseat and into the driver's seat!

Anyone who has experienced the loss of a partner or loved one knows it can be one of the most painful experiences a person will ever encounter in life. The emotions surrounding that loss can be debilitating even when you are intellectually prepared. But no matter how sympathetic your creditors are, they will still want your payments on time. Grief impairs your judgment and ability to understand how to best make all the decisions that lie ahead. Waiting until the time comes when you are forced to learn about how to handle your finances is not only a mistake, it's a tragedy.

Consider Hannah's dilemma. She was a stay-at-home mom and had been married to her husband, Paul, for seventeen years when he unexpectedly died from a massive heart attack. They were both in their early forties, and she was left with three children to care for. Their marriage was traditional in that she worked inside the home while he worked outside and handled all of their finances. Like many families, Hannah and Paul lived the good life. They owned an expensive home in a good neighborhood, sent their kids to private schools, drove luxury cars, and enjoyed frequent vacations to exotic locations. Hannah assumed that since Paul was a smart businessman in so many ways, he had prepared for the unexpected.

When he died, Hannah learned what it meant to belong to a class called the working rich. The term refers to those couples who can afford almost anything they want as long as at least one of them is working and earning a good salary, but who can no longer afford to live the same lifestyle when there's an unexpected change in earnings (through death, layoff, divorce, etc.). What Hannah hadn't realized was that despite the fact that Paul earned in excess of $200,000 annually, they were using nearly all of it for their day-to-day living expenses. He hadn't been saving, hadn't purchased a life insurance policy, and had left his family in the lurch.

No one can know what went into Paul's thinking, since he and Hannah never discussed family finances, but assuming he was like many young men, he probably thought he had many years left to plan for the future. At forty-two years old he most likely also felt that he was invincible. After all, he was healthy, wealthy (at least in the present), and wise. Perhaps he had come from a poor family and wanted to give his wife and children everything he never had. Or maybe he just had low impulse control, spending money as soon as he earned it. We don't really know why he didn't plan, but we do know that Hannah was as much to blame as Paul in this situation. By doing just a few simple things, she could have been left better equipped to handle the daunting emotional and financial task she faced after Paul died.

COACHING TIPS

• **Have the difficult discussion now.** People don't like to talk about what will happen in the event of death, because doing so causes them to face their own mortality. Not having it, however, leaves you unprepared to handle what needs to be taken care of at a time when you are under the most stress. Ongoing discussions will also prepare you to handle financial matters in the event of incapacitation or divorce. Talk to your partner about preparing a will or trust, how assets are to be distributed, and how to handle funeral arrangements. Similarly, discuss your family's current financial situation and investments. Learn about these fundamentals:

- Is there a life insurance policy? If not, why not? Is this a good time to purchase one?
- Is there a safe-deposit box? If so, where is it, what's in it, and where's the key?
- Where are the checkbooks kept?
- Who is the family attorney, accountant, and financial planner?
- In what financial institutions are assets held? Are there passwords to access them?
- Are you listed as a cosigner on all accounts? If not, how do you add your name?
- Where are the family financial records and will or trust kept?

You can also do a Web search for "financial planning booklets" to find places that will send you more information free of charge.

Mistake 12

Managing Egos, Not Your Wealth

$\mathcal{A}$s we all know, the male ego is a fragile thing. We tiptoe around difficult issues, avoid necessary questions, and acquiesce to decisions all in the name of preserving a man's ego. In the process, we watch them go down paths that may not be in our best interest and squander our hard-earned money. Is this *their* fault? Of course not! It's we who are playing the "nice girl" game and taking better care of them than we are taking care of ourselves. Let me share a case in point.

Delores is a successful physician with a large, thriving practice. She is well respected in her specialty area, trusted by her patients and colleagues alike, and earns nearly $300,000 annually. Delores is married to a stay-at-home dad who cares for the children quite well, the house so-so, and her finances miserably. The few times she questioned her husband's investment of the money *she* earned, he became so belligerent and pouted for so long that she made the decision it wasn't worth creating problems in the marriage. So she now leaves the finances totally up to him and focuses on earning enough money so that it won't matter if he loses some of it.

It's not only traditional, married couples who face this problem. It can also be women who trust their finances to boyfriends, business or life partners, parents, siblings, or financial advisers of either gender. Many women have told me that when they've questioned their financial advisers, they get the same response. The woman is somehow made to feel she couldn't possibly know what she is talking about or that she is in some way impugning the man's integrity. At best, "nice girls" will back down and avoid making any waves. At worst, they will believe that they probably don't know what they're talking about and develop "learned help-lessness."

Whether it's your money or joint money that's being imprudently invested, whether it's your spouse's ego or some other guy's, it's *your* financial future that's on the line. You've heard the saying "The best defense is a good offense." Well, this is precisely the attitude men take when their judgment is questioned or when they're feeling insecure about their ability to provide for their families. They go on the offensive, making you feel as if you've done something wrong or don't know what you're talking about. Don't relinquish your say in financial matters in order to avoid bruised egos. If you do, you'll only lengthen the time it takes you to become finan-cially free.

COACHING TIPS

- **Separate the act from the actor.** It's not about managing an ego, it's about managing a portfolio. When you discuss money matters, focus exclusively on the facts, not on the per-sonalities. If the other person wants to turn it into something personal, get in the habit of saying, "This is not about you. It's about the portfolio and finding ways to make it grow."
- **Recognize "arm's length" tactics.** They're exactly that—designed to keep you at a distance. Picking an argument, crit-icizing your knowledge, and bullying you into submission are all arm's length tactics. If you can identify these behaviors as tactics, you'll be more likely to stand up for yourself than if you look at them as personal assaults on your character.
- **Enlist the support of a neutral, outside party.** When you reach a stalemate, suggest getting input from a knowledgeable

professional (not a friend or family member) who can help the two of you make an objective decision. Again, focus on the problem, not the person.

- **Recognize and address negative reinforcement.** Eleanor Roosevelt once said, "No one can make you feel inferior without your consent." "Nice girls" collude with others who would like to keep them ignorant—about money or anything else, for that matter. Adult women don't give their consent. Instead, they take control of their lives by taking responsibility for learning about the matters that impact their lives. If requests to be included in financial discussions or educated about financial matters in your family are ignored, then it's up to you to find alternative methods for empowering yourself with the knowledge you need to create wealth.

Mistake 13

Not Trusting Your Intuition

*M*any of the women we spoke with cited doubting their own intuition as a major impediment to attaining financial independence. Most often it's because someone else is giving them advice, and they think this person surely knows more than they do. Here are just a few examples from women we spoke with related to this common mistake:

When I was eighteen, I had my first real forty-hour-per-week job. When I saw how much was being taken out in taxes, I spoke with my boyfriend about it. He told me to change my W-4 from one dependent to five dependents. This seemed odd to me, but I figured he knew what he was talking about. When I got my first paycheck, I was ecstatic—although it seemed too good to be true. When I prepared my taxes for that year, I did it three times and even had my uncle who is a CPA check it out. I swore I couldn't possibly owe the government $2,000 in taxes—but I did. I should have trusted my instincts that if it seems too good to be true, it probably is.

I once had a lawyer help our son in a custody fight. The lawyer kept failing and exhibited bouts of flakiness. I knew he was a loser, but my stepson thought he was the best choice we had. In the end the lawyer got disbarred, I was out $40,000, and my stepson is now using legal aid.

I was dating a guy who liked to dabble in stock market investments. He supposedly found a stock that was a sure thing and asked me to go in half with him. Against my better judgment I wrote him a check for $5,000. The investment went south, he got to write off the loss of $10,000, and I got nothing.

Have you ever noticed that the world values "gut feeling" more than "intuition"? One woman told me that she has learned to say "my gut tells me" as a means of giving her intuition the credibility and clout it deserves. Call it guts or intuition, when it comes to decisions related to finances, career, or making a major purchase, women are quick to second-guess their instincts and put their fate in the hands of someone else who may or may not know more than they do. As I tell women all the time, intuition isn't infallible, but it does usually have some basis in fact. Intuition is a sum total of our experiences, education, observations, and feelings. As such, it is something to be honored and listened to. The more you use it, the more finely tuned it becomes.

COACHING TIPS

- **Trust your intuition.** If your instincts tell you something seems too good to be true, it probably is. Get-rich-quick schemes aren't your best bet when it comes to planning your financial future. Some of them may actually pan out for some people, but the question to ask yourself is, "Can I afford to lose this investment?" If the answer is no, don't do it. On the other hand, don't avoid risks entirely or discount what might be a great opportunity. If you're in a position where losing a few hundred or even a few thousand dollars won't hurt you in the long run, you may want to take a stab at grasping the brass ring. In short, trust your gut and don't immediately dismiss potentially profitable ventures. Take calculated risks.

• **Don't be afraid to say "no thanks."** There are times when our intuition tells us no, no, no and our lips say yes, yes, yes. It's usually when we're emotionally involved with the person making the request. If someone makes you feel guilty about not doing what he or she thinks is a great idea, hold your ground. You can always say something like, "It's not that I'm saying it's a bad idea, I'm only saying I don't feel comfortable going in that direction at this time." You don't even have to give a reason. And say "no thanks" as many times as you have to until the person gets the message.

• **Call a time-out.** When your intuition puts up a red flag, it's time to ask questions, but those questions may not come to you immediately. Don't succumb to someone else's sense of urgency. If you're not convinced something is a good idea, ask for time to sleep on it or to do more research on it. Be skeptical of anyone who tells you this opportunity may not last for long. Even if it doesn't, there's another one out there—one that you may be more comfortable with.

• **Recognize those times when it's best to do nothing.** The weeks and months following a significant loss, including death, divorce, or the incapacitation of a loved one, are fraught with emotions. We typically do not make our best decisions under circumstances such as these. Avoid the inclination to immediately put your house on the market, cash in all your savings, and move to the south of France, or trust the first person who comes along who says he or she can give you all the help you need. Give yourself a set period of time to grieve and heal before focusing on financial matters. Your own situation will dictate how long this can be, so be aware of how much time you can take before having to return to the reality of financial decision making.

Mistake 14

Trusting the Wrong People

*W*omen who inherit money upon the death of a spouse or loved one—or acquire it after a divorce—are particularly vulnerable to trusting the wrong people. In either situation they may be feeling emotionally fragile and willingly fall prey to the first person (usually a man) who pays attention to them. The investment advisers I spoke with shared horror stories about women who inherit large amounts of money only to trust the wrong person and have it disappear. One elderly woman inherited several million dollars from a husband who had planned well for her financial future. Not long after he passed away she found herself being courted by a charming gentleman who assured her he had expertise in managing portfolios of this size. She was flattered by the attention and relieved to have someone step in and take over where her husband left off. Without checking it out, she blindly trusted him and in less than three years found herself living alone in a one-bedroom apartment without the financial security her husband had carefully ensured for her.

It's not only the elderly woman or divorcée who makes the wrong choices about whom to listen to. Many women reported listening to well-meaning or know-it-all boyfriends, coworkers, or family members who had get-rich-quick schemes for them. In each case the woman regretted not getting more information before she entrusted or invested her money, and cited this particular mistake as a major reason she wasn't financially independent at this stage of her life. I made this same mistake once when I was referred to a stockbroker who supposedly achieved phenomenal results for a friend of mine.

She couldn't say enough positive things about the man. I decided to give him $10,000 to invest for me, then I promptly forgot about it.

About nine months later when I finally took the time to look at my monthly statement, I saw he actually lost $3,000 of my money—and this was during the dot-com boom when *everyone* was making money. During the time I worked with him I even called him and asked him to buy some new stock called Amazon.com and was told it was too risky. Although he didn't buy the Amazon stock for me (which would have significantly increased my portfolio), he did manage to buy and sell other speculative stocks that consistently lost money. Since stockbrokers make their commissions on the sale and purchase of individual stocks, he was engaging in a practice called churning—frequently buying and selling small amounts of stock, thereby increasing his fees. As I said in a letter to him when I fired him, "Someone is making money here but it obviously isn't me."

COACHING TIPS

Financial adviser and author Nick Murray writes, "A relationship based on the performance of investments is no relationship at all and must ultimately end badly, but a relationship based on faith and trust of a financial consultant can last forever." During the course of writing this book I met two highly motivated, savvy women who work with affluent clients and have tremendous insight and experience related to establishing and maintaining successful business relationships. Karen Blanchard and Maureen Kerrigan, financial consultants with the Stanek/Blanchard Group at RBC Dain Rauscher in Hartford, Connecticut, provide these suggestions for you to consider:

- **Select an adviser you trust.** Don't think of it as selecting a stockbroker, think of it as a relationship you're going to be in—hopefully for a long time. The basis for any financial relationship is trust, and results alone don't mean you should trust someone.

- **Select someone with a broad base of knowledge.** It does no good to amass a fortune when you don't have a plan in place detailing how you want your estate distributed or if you don't have the right health, disability, or life insurance to protect your assets in the event of illness or medical catastrophe. Consideration of these factors is an integral part of your well-being. A good financial consultant (or more appropriately, a "wealth manager") will ensure you transfer your wealth as you desire and by the most efficient means possible, *not* just sell you stocks, bonds, and mutual funds. Blanchard and Kerrigan perceive their role as that of a relationship manager, working with clients to manage expectations and assisting them in channeling "financial emotion" in a positive, constructive way.

- **Ask yourself whether you leave an interview more informed than when you went in.** Blanchard and Kerrigan emphasize the importance of education, not just management of money. The goal isn't always to turn your money over to someone else and expect him or her to grow it for you. You have the option to be a partner in the process, and part of that process is increasing knowledge and understanding that will enhance your comfort level. If you feel as if you're in a sales meeting where the potential adviser is doing more talking than listening, consider this a red flag.

- **Ask for a complimentary consultation.** Some investment firms charge a fee to meet with you and review your portfolio, whereas others are willing to do this at no charge. Why? Because the latter operate with the belief that educating you, understanding your needs, and developing trust are vital for a successful financial relationship and that once these are in place, the firm's compensation won't be far behind.

- **Inquire about commissions/fees/expenses.** Do not hesitate to review the cost of services. Although fee-based advisers do charge a percentage of your total portfolio, those fees may be tax-deductible.* Conversely, when you buy a mutual fund or a proprietary product from an investment firm, it may seem as if there are no fees, but the adviser is more than likely getting a commission from the sale. Again, this isn't to say one is better than the other; just don't hesitate to ask for a clear (and preferably written) explanation about what the exact fees are and how the professional is compensated for his or her services. "The fees should be transparent, and the process one that incorporates an open-architecture best-in-class approach," say Blanchard and Kerrigan.

*RBC Dain Rauscher does not provide tax or legal advice. All decisions regarding the tax or legal implications of your investments should be made in connection with your independent tax or legal adviser.

Mistake 15

Living Together Before Discussing Finances

 I recently had a woman cabdriver in New York (one of the few) complain that whenever she lived with a guy she never had any money and when she lived alone she had plenty of discretionary cash. Although she wasn't exactly sure why this happened, she had a hunch it had something to do with the fact that she seemed to pick chronically unemployed men who were more than happy to have her take care of them. Oy. Why is it that so many women need so desperately to take care of someone that they'll fork over money to do it? The need for affiliation, being raised to be "givers," and viewing money as a means, not necessarily an end are but three answers to that question.

Whether you're twenty-five or seventy-five, there's nothing wrong with living together. And there's nothing wrong with helping your partner get through a difficult spell. Any one of us would want the same in return. But when the rough patch lasts more than a few weeks and when it happens over and over, it's no longer a rough patch—and you've got to take a look at the way in which you're sabotaging your own well-being. This is what makes it critically important to talk about how money will be spent, saved, and pooled *before* you move in together. If you're a "nice girl," you might feel somewhat brash when you initiate the conversation, but no one who truly loves you and wants the best for you should resent you for broaching this important subject. And trust me, if the relationship doesn't work out, you'll thank your lucky stars you had the courage to converse about it beforehand.

COACHING TIPS

• **Read** *Shacking Up: The Smart Girl's Guide to Living in Sin without Getting Burned,* by Stacey Whitman and Wynne Whitman (Broadway Books, 2003). This witty and wise book, written by two sisters, contains more than just financial advice. It covers everything from things to consider before you cohabit to legal matters that impact live-ins.

• **Discuss asset, debt, and earnings protection.** Freelance writer MP Dunleavy claims the biggest mistake she ever made—both financially and emotionally—was moving cross-country to live with her boyfriend before having discussed key financial issues. Moving in together may seem like a terrific idea when you're pining for each other, but as Dunleavy points out, "Cohabiting couples will often embark on all kind of financial entwinements—joint bank accounts, joint credit cards, joint purchases of big-ticket items . . . without batting an eye." You've got to talk about (1) who owns what, (2) who will repay debt that is mutually incurred, and (3) how you will divvy up the household expenses. It may seem unromantic to do it this way, but you can wind up losing a considerable amount of your resources if you don't.

• **Keep a savings and/or checking account of your own.** It's not a matter of trust, it's a matter of money. In addition to any joint monies you have, you want to have your own account. Plenty of cohabiting or married couples (myself included) do this. In most relationships there's inequality in terms of earnings, and it's simply not fair for either of you to live beyond your means. As Elizabeth Cady Stanton said, "Every woman should have her own purse."

Mistake 16

Letting a Deadbeat Dad Shirk His Responsibility

*T*here are plenty of reasons why a woman won't pursue a former husband or partner who fails to pay his fair share of raising a child. Three of the most common reasons are not wanting to create animosity between herself and the father of her children, not having the emotional strength for a lengthy (and costly) legal battle, and being hesitant to damage the relationship with in-laws who have become family to her. If you fall into one of these categories, you've got to consider how your failure to act is impacting not only your kids but your financial future as well. Given the fact that you're expected to live longer and earn less over your lifetime and that you're less likely to have enough money to retire, you're putting yourself in financial danger.

According to a recent U.S. Census Bureau report:

- Of the 14 million parents awarded custody of children under the age of twenty-one, approximately 85 percent were women and 15 percent were men.
- Only about two-thirds (67.4 percent) of the custodial parents who were due child support received either full or partial payments.
- Less than half ever received the full amount of their court-ordered child support payments.
- Noncustodial parents owe nearly $30 billion, whether by court order or settled upon out of court. Mothers were due nearly 90 percent of that money.

Clearly, the burden of child support among divorced couples falls squarely on the shoulders of more women than men. Getting financial support for your children isn't always easy, but objectifying the matter and removing the emotions that prevent you from pursuing the matter can help. It's no longer just about your relationship with your former partner, it's about what's fair, just, and right.

COACHING TIPS

- **Enlist emotional support.** Many times your friends and family members can see the situation far more objectively than you can. Make it clear that you don't want to engage in ex-husband bashing, but you do want emotional support for getting financial relief. That support can take the form of going to an attorney with you, being present when you call your ex for past-due payments, or just listening to you. If you find that friends and family can't be objective, seek professional counseling.

- **Buy a term life insurance policy.** Be certain that you are named as the beneficiary. This will prevent it from being changed without your permission.

- **Keep good records.** Keep a payment log that shows when a payment is made, what date(s) you contacted your ex to remind him of overdue payments, and how much was actually paid. This will ensure you have adequate documentation in the event you have to take legal action.

- **Use appropriate enforcement agencies.** Anyone can get into a financial bind now and then. Reporting a former spouse for being a few weeks late on child support payments, particularly when he's been timely in the past, can serve to fuel a fire. If you've waited a reasonable amount of time, however, and have shown due diligence in trying to collect the money on your own, then take action. Federal law provides for reporting on any amount due that exceeds $1,000. Some agencies that can be of help to you are National Child Support Enforcement Association at www.ncsea.org. and Administration for Children and Families at www.acf.dhhs.gov/programs/cse. You can also contact your district attorney and ask for help with securing the money through liens, Social Security benefits, or retirement fund annuities.

Mistake 17

Not Attending to Your Existing Material Assets

*I*deally, every woman would have someone to help her handle life's many mundane tasks. Someone to make sure the gardener is doing his job, be at home to meet the roofer, or bring the car in for a tire rotation. We are so busy taking care of everyone else's needs and assets that we often neglect our own. One of the most common ways in which women do this is to run their cars into the ground because they don't have the time or don't want to take the time to have it serviced. As a result, they are faced with costly repair bills that could have been avoided with a little time and attention.

A woman with whom we spoke shared the story of how she knew her washing machine was leaking but she didn't want to take the time off from work to meet the repairman. Pretty soon the floor beneath the washer had dry rot and ultimately termites. What should have been a hundred-dollar repair bill turned into thousands of dollars for home repair costs. And it's not just cars and homes that we neglect. We don't find the time to take that expensive dress sitting in the closet to the tailor for alterations, we don't have our physical fitness equipment (bikes, treadmills, etc.) serviced, and we don't call the guy to repair the sprinklers until the lawn and shrubbery are dead and need replacing. All because we've put our own priorities at the bottom of the to-do list.

COACHING TIPS

- **Take stock of your material assets.** We often don't even think about the things we've acquired as assets. We take them for granted. You've worked hard for your home, car, and other necessities and niceties. Consider them as part of your portfolio the same as you would other investments.

- **Take a personal business day to protect your assets.** With a little effort you can schedule the people you need to give an estimate for necessary home repairs, bring your car in for service, and get to the tailor—all on the same day. If this doesn't qualify as personal business, what does?

- **At the beginning of each year, schedule regular maintenance activities.** Rather than writing down new year's resolutions that you're not going to keep, use that time to take your calendar and schedule the times when you're going to bring your car in for service, have your home air conditioner inspected, or get a tune-up for your bicycle. Writing commitments on the calendar increases the likelihood that you will actually make them happen.

- **Protect yourself from identity theft.** The rise in identity theft over the past several years has been phenomenal. The Federal Trade Commission's Identity Theft Hotline received more than 16,000 calls since it opened in 1999 and anticipates that will grow to more than 200,000 in the next few years. MasterCard alone reports more than $407 million in fraudulent activity. A friend of mine who test-drove a car gave her credit information at the request of the salesperson only to find that someone from the dealership stole her identity and started making purchases on her credit cards. The U.S. Department of Education suggests that you keep close tabs on to whom and why you give out personal credit information and that you follow these suggestions:

- Memorize your Social Security number and passwords. Don't record your passwords on papers you carry with you.
- Don't use your date of birth as your password.
- Shred pre-approved credit applications and other financial documents before discarding them.
- Order credit reports every year from each of the major credit reporting agencies and thoroughly review them for accuracy. Recent legislation allows you to do so at no charge once a year.
- Never give personal or financial information over the phone or Internet unless you initiated the contact.
- Don't carry your Social Security card or birth certificate with you.
- Report lost or stolen credit cards immediately.
- Check your monthly credit card and bank statements for unusual activity.
- Use a firewall program on your computer, especially if you leave your computer connected to the Internet twenty-four hours a day.
- Do not download files sent to you by strangers or click on hyperlinks from people you don't know.

There are numerous companies that, for a fee (usually between fifteen and fifty dollars annually), will alert you when there is unusual activity on your credit cards or when a credit check is done against your identity. Unfortunately, many of these companies are as unscrupulous as the practice itself. I suggest you go to www.consumerreports.org/main and click on "consumer protection" to research the companies they recommend.

- **Hire people to help.** If it's necessary, pay someone to take care of your physical assets. Ask your housekeeper to come an extra day to meet a repairman, or pay a neighborhood kid to water the lawn while you're out of town.

Mistake 18

Not Taking Care of Your Most Important Asset: You

*H*ave you ever noticed how many more men work out regularly than women? Especially women who are married or who have kids. There's a reason for this. Women just don't have (or don't carve out) the time needed to stay healthy. Don't get the idea that I'm one of those physical fitness nuts, because I'm not. In fact, I have to push myself to get to the gym once a week if I'm lucky. But when I am there, I have the most wonderful sense of well-being. I know I'm doing something good for myself—not anyone else, just me. When I leave, I always feel better prepared to engage in whatever challenges face me that day.

It's not just in the area of physical activity that women short shrift themselves. How many times have you canceled or postponed a regular dental appointment because you didn't think you could spare the time? How much did it cost you in dental work that wouldn't have been necessary had you kept your regularly scheduled visits? Women who wouldn't think of missing a hairdresser appointment often find themselves in physical or emotional pain because they won't take the time to see a health care professional.

What does this have to do with getting rich? you ask. As I've said before, getting rich is in large part about how you *think*. One study conducted by the Center for the Study of Aging found, "The ability of individuals to reach and secure an independent income for their advanced years can be greatly affected by the condition of their health over their lifetime." Taking care of your body and mind is essential to having the physical and emotional stamina needed to earn, manage, and enjoy your wealth. What good does it do to meet your financial goals if you don't have health to go along with it? I, for one, want to enjoy my wealth—both physically and emotionally.

COACHING TIPS

• **Schedule your annual physical, mammogram, or gynecological exam around your birthday.** Using this annual event provides a good reminder that it's time to make that call—and it's a great way to celebrate *you*. And while you're at it, remind your friends to do the same. When a friend of mine schedules her yearly mammogram, she sends a funny notice called "Bosom Buddies" to the women she cares about to encourage them to do the same.

• **Join a gym.** If you're intimidated by traditional gyms, work out with a video, on your own, or check out Curves—a unique gym for women. Their program is a thirty-minute workout that's fun, relatively easy, and inexpensive. Although it was designed primarily for women over forty, I see lots of younger women there too. If you travel a lot on business, they'll even give you a card good for use at facilities other than the one in your hometown. You can learn more about the program and find one near you by going to their Web site: www.curvesinternational.com.

• **Take a hike.** Getting in mental shape to get rich can be as simple as taking a walk a couple of times a week. It can be a lot easier when you've got a friend to do it with, so why not ask a neighbor or colleague at work to walk with you three times a week? And while you're walking, talk about how you're going to get rich.

- **Take your next vacation at a health spa.** Pamper yourself and jump-start your physical fitness regimen at the same time. There are spas to meet everyone's budget, so don't assume you can't afford it. Indulge yourself by going to www.spafinder. com and checking out the many different types of experiences available.

- **Get a hobby.** For me, nothing beats a day spent in the garden for rejuvenating my mind and body. Photography, painting, cooking, and any number of other pastimes are the perfect antidotes for a busy life.

Chapter Four

Spending Your Money Wisely

Whoever said money can't buy happiness simply didn't know where to go shopping.

BO DEREK

I just know there's a shopping gene because I inherited one from my mother. It was the only hobby of which she would regularly partake. When it came to shopping endurance, she could outlast any Olympian. And, like my mother, I shop to relieve stress, to fill unscheduled time between appointments, soothe an emotional hurt, celebrate a success . . . well, you get the picture. In my opinion, there's really no *bad* time to shop. Nonetheless, indiscriminate spending is a huge impediment to achieving financial goals. Consider these facts:

- In the year 2000 the United States was the only country where a higher percentage of online shoppers were women—60 percent—than men. (Ernst & Young, 2001)
- Single women spend a larger percentage of their income than single men—even though men earn more and their overall dollar expenditure is higher. According to the Consumer Expenditure Survey, the average income of the male

one-person household is $28,500, and his average annual spending is $23,700. The average female one-person household income is $20,800, and her average annual spending is $20,600.

- Women are far more likely than men (1) to buy without need or buy things they know they don't need, (2) to use shopping as a method of celebration, (3) to purchase unplanned items, and (4) to buy things as often as possible. The spending habits of women are more likely than those of men to create chaos in their lives. (*Journal of Financial Planning*, February 2000)

And what accounts for these differences in spending? Jay Macdonald, writing for Bankrate.com, says, "From birth women and men are raised to view and spend money quite differently. Our behavior is based primarily on what was modeled by our same-sex parent." Although Macdonald acknowledges that money paradigms are changing, it's still true that "women view money as a means to create a lifestyle and spend on things that enhance day-to-day living. Men view money as a means to capture and accumulate value. They don't spend, they invest."

What makes taking control of spending so difficult is a bit the same as what makes taking control of your eating habits so hard. You have to eat, so it's not like you can completely stop eating or ignore food. It's always in front of you, so if you need to control your eating, you have to exercise willpower. And food does nurture and sustain you, so in itself eating is not a bad thing. The same is true for spending. There are things you legitimately need to buy, but in the process you will see things you don't need but would *like* to buy, and so willpower becomes an issue here too. Spending isn't such a bad thing either. It's all about how you spend. Just as a diet or willpower alone won't help you keep off the weight you may lose, a budget alone won't get you rich. Consider this chapter an introduction to a whole new approach to how you spend money. Recognizing the mistakes you make with regard to spending is the first step toward getting control over it. It's not about abstaining entirely from spending money, it's about doing it with intention and doing it wisely.

Mistake 19

Getting into Deep Debt

*T*his is one of the most fatal mistakes you can make on the road to abundance. It's like digging a hole, climbing in, and not being able to get out. It colors all other aspects of your life including your health, long-term financial security, career decisions, interactions in relationships, and a general sense of well-being. But I don't have to tell you that—you already know it. The real question is, why do we do it? Why do we spend more than we have? Why do so many people walk around with a dark cloud called debt hanging over their heads? The answers to these questions vary from person to person, but see if one or more of these reasons apply to you:

- Guilt: "If I can't spend enough time with [fill in the name of a loved one or close friend], I can at least buy them something I know they'd really like."
- Envy: "Someone else (often less deserving) has it—why shouldn't I?"
- Living in the moment: "You only go around once—and you can't take it with you."
- Impulsiveness: "I just can't control myself when I get into a mall."
- Appearances: "If I don't drive a Mercedes, people will think I'm not successful."
- Low self-esteem: "I'll feel like a better person if I buy dinner for everyone."
- Emotional fulfillment: "I'm not in a good relationship, I'm not happy, and spending makes me feel better."

- Available credit: "I wouldn't have been given this credit line if they didn't think I could pay it back."

Mary Rowland, an author and frequent contributor to MSN.money, reports that research into why people accumulate debt has more to do with their self-esteem than it has to do with how much they earn. She has found that nearly 25 percent of those with money problems require psychological counseling in addition to professional financial advice.

COACHING TIPS

- **Use only cash for one week.** Professor Tahira Hira, a researcher from Iowa State University, claims that most people have no idea how much they spend in a week or a month because they charge so many of their purchases. If you have to pay cash for everything you buy, you're more likely to think twice before letting the money slip through your fingers.
- **Use only one credit card.** Keep the card with the lowest interest rate and no annual fee or (if you're a frequent traveler) the one that gives you the most air miles. Cut up the rest. I challenge you to get up right now, open your wallet, pull out your cards, and cut up all but one of them. You don't need Nordstrom, Sears, the Home Depot, JCPenney, and Bloomingdale's cards (to name a few). One all-purpose Visa or MasterCard will do the trick. Okay, okay. If you use your card for business, you can have two—one for your personal expenses and one for business expenses. More than that is too much temptation for many people.
- **Pay off all credit card charges each month.** Although some credit agencies suggest that debt of 10 to 20 percent of

your monthly income is acceptable, financial adviser Katherine Wimmer says, "The maximum amount of credit card debt that someone should carry is *zero*! No balances should be allowed to accumulate. Credit cards are an expensive way to finance purchases. *Pay as you go.*"

• **Make one trip per week to the ATM.** Determine how much cash you need for the week, make one trip to the ATM, and take out exactly that amount. When the cash is gone, your spending is done.

• **Negotiate with your credit card company.** Many companies are willing to give you a better rate or eliminate your annual fee, if you only ask. Use the length of time you've been with them, offers from other companies, and the threat of closing your account as leverage.

• **If you're already in debt, get out as quickly as possible.** Consider accelerating payments or negotiating with credit card companies to develop a repayment schedule. Wimmer suggests that in extreme cases people should contact the National Foundation for Credit Counseling at www.nfcc.org or 800-388-2227.

Mistake 20

Spending as an Emotional Crutch

*T*here are two kinds of emotional spending. One is the purchase that is so personally appealing to you that it plays on your emotions and results in an "I've gotta have it" buy. The other is the use of money for emotional comfort. This mistake addresses the latter, and I'll address the former in the next section. Although not all women are equally likely to fall victim to this mistake, they are more likely than men to engage in it. The following comment received from one of the women we surveyed is reflective of many we received:

> I would buy things based on my emotional state at the time. If I was sad, or feeling rejected, or wanting a boyfriend, I would go out and purchase something with the hope of feeling better. Ten pairs of shoes. Let's make it fifteen! A new blouse to impress a guy I had my eye on—still didn't work.

Emotional spending is a short-term fix to a long-term problem. Author and motivational speaker Valorie Burton reminds us, "If you remain on a path controlled by your emotions you will never enjoy the emotional, spiritual, and financial life you were meant to have. The first step to eliminating poor financial choices and making smart financial choices is to identify the emotions that are sabotaging you."

Consider whether any of these emotions are the real culprit for you: anger, jealousy, loneliness, fear, shame, or hopelessness. The inability to address or perhaps even identify the emotions that cause you to make emotional purchases contributes significantly to your continuing down this expensive path. That's why each coaching tip is more psychologically than behaviorally oriented.

COACHING TIPS

• **Do some soul-searching.** Burton advises you to answer these two questions: In what ways are my emotions preventing me from achieving the financial success I desire, and what am I willing to do about it? Write your answers down on paper. Refer back to them when you have the urge to make an emotional splurge.

• **Don't shop when you're feeling most vulnerable.** It's a quick fix. It may make you feel better in the moment, but you're only avoiding the inevitable need to deal with whatever it is that's causing you to feel this way.

• **Thwart the impulse to spend.** Even if you do so only momentarily, you will find a flood of emotions arise that will provide clues to your emotional spending. Once you can understand what's going on inside, you'll be better able to handle the external manifestation of these feelings.

• **Seek professional psychological help.** If destructive emotions are ruling your life, you owe it to yourself to invest in creating a healthier emotional and financial future. The money you spend on a therapist will pay off in dividends that will far exceed emotional spending.

Mistake 21

Making Emotionally Driven Purchases

My husband and I fell in love with a house and made an offer on the spot. A week into the escrow process we discovered that the square footage of the house had been overstated by six hundred feet. We wanted the house so badly that we didn't ask for a reduction in price. We bought the house at the height of the real estate market in our neighborhood and when we sold it several years later, took a $35,000 loss. We would not have had that loss if we hadn't been so emotional over the purchase.

*F*rom collectibles to vacation time-shares, most of us have had the same experience as the one reported by this woman: We make a major purchase, then realize we made a mistake. Buyer's remorse doesn't belong only in the domain of purchasing a home. Doing almost anything in an emotionally driven state can result in later remorse. Although women don't have the corner on the emotional purchasing market, they do have a sizable piece of the territory. Whether it's an emotional drive to marry prematurely or purchase a car you test-drove because it makes you feel sexy, not thinking it through logically and realistically is often a mistake you later live to regret. Considering the following coaching tips can help you avoid making emotionally driven purchases too often.

COACHING TIPS

- **Get input from an experienced friend or family member.** Before making a major purchase, ask for input from people who have been down the same road. It doesn't mean you have to follow their advice, but you also don't have to reinvent the wheel. Sometimes their experiences can help prevent you from making a huge financial mistake.

- **Call a time-out.** This is especially true when buying a home, a car, or other big-ticket item from someone who stands to gain a significant amount of money from your purchase. If you're going to spend whatever you consider to be a large amount of money, you don't have to do it in the time frame the salesperson wants. Go home, think about it, and do some research. Sometimes just the time-out is enough to break the emotional connection such that you don't feel obsessed to make the purchase, or it gives you the chance to realize that you don't really need the item. One of the most profitable time-outs that I ever called was when I was negotiating for a new car that I wanted so badly I almost blew it. The dealer wanted more than I planned to pay, so I left the showroom knowing this was not the end of the negotiation, and even if it was, there were other car dealers in town. I went home, and by the end of the evening, he had called me to negotiate a more reasonable price.

- **Never cash in savings or retirement funds for emotionally driven purchases.** This is a mistake you will most definitely come to regret. The money in your savings and retirement accounts grows through compounding. By withdrawing that money, you don't only spend the actual amount taken out of the account, you lose the hundreds (or thousands) of dollars you would have accrued if you had left the money there. If you've been saving for an expensive purchase and you think you've found exactly what you want, it won't hurt to wait a day or two to be certain that emotions aren't the driver—*you* are.

• **Beware of financing on emotionally driven purchases.** If common sense has left your head over the purchase, then it won't be there when it comes to how much you're going to pay in interest. Before spending, think about whether financing the payment is actually worth it. One woman told us, "In the end I must have paid $1,000 for that $400 Kirby vacuum cleaner I just had to have after the salesman demonstrated it for me." The same holds true of the "extras" that are suddenly available, such as extended warranties, special attachments, and prepaid maintenance agreements.

• **Don't leave a deposit or arrange for immediate delivery.** These are two techniques salespeople are taught to use in an effort to avoid having you delay or reconsider a purchase. The deposit binds you to them for just that much longer, and immediate delivery ensures you won't change your mind during a cooling-off period.

• **Understand the psychology of the "30-day free in-home trial."** After they deliver and set up that new treadmill, the mattress with massaging pillow, or surround-sound stereo system, do you really think you're going to disassemble it all and send it back? Of course not. Neither does the seller. It's why they're so quick to tell you if you're not 100 percent satisfied, you can send it back. You'll notice they don't say they'll come and get it! As an alternative, locate outlets that sell the item you're considering buying. If there's a showroom, stop in to test out your potential purchase, *then* consider buying it.

• **Consider how many hours you will have to work to pay for that purchase.** In the book *Your Money or Your Life* (Penguin, 1992) authors Joe Dominguez and Vicki Robin suggest you calculate your hourly wage and when considering a purchase, divide that wage into the cost of the item to determine how many hours it will take you to earn that amount. When you figure it that way, you might be more likely to walk away.

Mistake 22

24/7 Shopping

*F*rom Internet shopping to infomercials, shopping channels, and all those catalogs that fill our mailboxes, the number of ways we can spend our money at any time of the day or night has increased exponentially over the past decade. The shopping channel sirens discounts, promises of speaking with celebrity hosts, and buying opportunities calibrated in minutes. Pop-up advertisements and spam may be annoying, but they obviously work or else they would have gone the route of the milkman. It's now possible to go shopping from the comfort of your own home without having to get dressed, when you can't sleep, when you're home sick, or when the weather is bad—and every time in between!

The Internet can be a wonderful time-saver—and as we all know, time is money. I've convinced myself that the time I save having to go to the hardware store to find that unique piece of gardening equipment is worth the extra money I spend online on other items I might not have purchased had I actually gone to the store. The illogic of this, however, is that I'm probably doing it at a time when I wouldn't have been earning money anyway!

And what about all those items you purchase using the one-click feature of certain Web sites? Their clever marketing scheme has made it practically impossible to walk away without buying something. Add in the "free shipping for purchases over $25.00" and you're like a rat caught in a maze. Internet shopping may have contributed to UPS stock climbing dramatically, but it hasn't done us "girls" any favors.

COACHING TIPS

- **Turn off the computer when you're finished doing actual work or checking e-mail.** You'll be less likely to power it up to go shopping.

- **Read a book.** Rather than use shopping on the Internet or watching the shopping channels for entertainment, pick up a book or magazine and start reading. Call me old-fashioned, but time spent with a good book is far more fulfilling—and safer—than surfing the shopping waves.

- **Set a limit.** If you're a home shopping channel or Internet shopping junkie, then at least set a spending limit. When you've reached that limit, put your credit card away.

- **Avoid sites that make it easy to spend.** If your name pops up with a welcome sign when you log on, take it as a sign you've visited too often.

- **Program the remote to not stop at shopping channels.** Need I say more about this one?

- **Read that catalog.** Go ahead and read it, mark the pages that have items of interest to you, then put the catalog away for a week or two (see how long you can resist picking it up again). When you do return to it, see if you still need those items as badly as you thought you did.

Mistake 23

Impulse Buying

$\mathscr{A}$ failing of many "nice girls" is the inability to manage impulse spending. In fact, one of the findings of a study conducted by Tahira K. Hira, PhD, and Olive Mugenda, PhD, was that women really do have less sales resistance than men. It's one of the reasons why pop-up ads, catalogs, and infomercials work so effectively on us. One woman we surveyed reported, "I have a catalog fetish! I just can't resist ordering things that I think will solve all my decorating or couture problems. Then I spend some real time at the post office returning them or, worse yet, taking them straight to Goodwill!" When it comes to impulse buying, merchandisers have it all over us. They know the psychology of shoppers, and willpower doesn't seem to have a prayer.

Sonia is another great example of an impulse buyer. She worked her entire career as a teacher, earning a modest salary and accumulating an even more modest retirement fund. On a hot and muggy Midwest July afternoon she blew it all on a decision to build a swimming pool in her backyard, liquidating her retirement account. In retrospect she knows it was a foolish thing to do, although at the time it seemed right. That's the problem with impulse buying: It's as if all reason leaves us, and we're left with an irresistible urge to have that pool or car or bracelet.

Think for a moment about the psychology of impulse buying. Have you ever noticed how stores put all those little "impulse buys" at the front counter? Or how clothing is displayed with the slacks, blouse, and sweater put together on a mannequin or hanger so you can see what the ensemble actually looks like? Furniture stores don't separate the couches, tables, and lamps—they put them together in a room display. Even the "special offer" coupons given to you at the checkout of the grocery store are geared to complement your other purchases. Retailers know that you're more likely to buy on impulse when you see how things go together or when you already have your wallet in hand. The following tips will help you fight those impulses the next time you go shopping.

COACHING TIPS

• **Read *Why We Buy: The Science of Shopping,*** by Paco Underhill (Simon & Schuster, 2000). It will give you insight into why you make certain unplanned purchases and, I hope, arm you with the information needed to avoid doing so in the future.

• **Make a list before you shop.** Dr. Jo Turner, a professor of family and consumer economics, reports that only three out of ten purchases are decided upon in advance, while about half of all purchases are made completely on impulse. Having a list in hand will allow you to focus on what you went out to actually buy and not what appears in the line of sight once you arrive.

• **Make it a habit to sleep on all purchases that exceed $250.** Again, don't deny yourself the right to think about it, but do think about it. The larger the purchase, the longer you should think. Use the time to consider why this purchase is important to you, whether you're getting the best deal, and whether it's needed or just wanted.

• **Keep only catalogs you've actually requested.** Throw out the rest. Trust me, you'll never miss them. Better yet, go to www.dmaconsumers.org and register to have your name removed from mailing lists.

Mistake 24

Guilt Shopping Trips

*D*oes this scenario sound familiar? Your best friend gave you a beautiful expensive handcrafted vase for Christmas last year. You thought you had an agreement to limit the cost for gifts to fifty dollars or less, so you gave her a sweater set you found on sale at Ann Taylor for just under the limit. After you opened the gifts, you were embarrassed by what seemed to be such a big difference in the value of them, so you decide you'll make up for it when her birthday rolls around.

How about this one? You've been spending a lot of time away from home on business lately, leaving your grade school children in the care of a nanny. Each city you go to, you make it a point to find a special gift to bring home to them. As hard as you try to choose just the right thing for each child, they don't seem to appreciate the thought or the gift. You wind up feeling even more guilty because you know they're just responding to your absence, not the gift.

Oy, guilt. It makes us do things we wouldn't normally do and buy things we certainly can't afford. From wanting the kids to be able to keep up with their classmates to wanting to meet your husband's desire to keep up with the neighbors, our guilt over not being able to provide as much as what we think others expect makes us spend more than we logically should. The important thing to remember about guilt is that it's self-imposed. Sure, people can try to make us feel guilty ("But, Mom, all of the kids are getting Mercedes CLKs for their sixteenth birthdays. I'll be the only kid without one"). But accepting it or rejecting it is totally our own choice.

It's important that you take a look at where your guilt

comes from. Do you want to give that guilt gift because you haven't visited your mother lately? Or because you yelled at your husband before he left for work? Guilt comes from regretting a decision we made or an action we took, but it is self-imposed and can't be corrected with spending.

COACHING TIPS

• **Consider alternatives to guilt gifts.** A homemade gift, freshly prepared meal, or time spent together can go just as long a way as a gift you really can't afford.

• **Talk about differences in gift giving.** Rather than assume the other person is disappointed with the less expensive gift he or she received from you, talk about your feelings. It could be that the other person is being extravagant due to his or her own difficult relationship with money or wants to share an unexpected windfall. If this is the case, you don't do either of you a favor by perpetuating the one-upmanship.

• **Set spending limits *before* holidays or gift-giving events.** Tell people that you feel blessed to have so much and ask that their gift to you be a donation to a charitable cause or simply a nice lunch. Let people know you are going to do the same. If they choose not to honor your request, so be it. But resist the urge to make up for it at a later time.

• **Don't try to compensate for time spent away from home earning a living by buying gifts.** No amount of money in the world can take the place of time spent with your family. Spending money on gifts, luxury vacations, or expensive restaurants doesn't change the feelings people have about what they would like from you. You're better off sitting down with the people who resent your absence and having a heart-to-heart discussion about how each of you can get your needs met in the context of a demanding job or work schedule.

Mistake 25

Making Up for Lost Time

*W*hen I was a little girl, Father always told us we were poor," said one woman now in her fifties. "We lived very frugally and I didn't have all the things other kids did. I just assumed it was how life was until my father died and my sisters and I inherited nearly $250,000 each. The first thing I did was go out and splurge on things I never thought I'd ever have. Before I knew it, most of the money was gone."

Stories like this one are not uncommon. Whether you're resentful because of what you never had or joyful because you can now have all the things you ever wanted, spending money to make up for lost time can sabotage your financial well-being. It's about filling up a hole that was created a long time ago; it is not about living in the moment. You can't make up for what you didn't have by frivolously spending money now.

Consider all the dot-com people who, working in high-tech businesses during the 1990s, earned huge sums of money early in their careers. Many were just out of college and had more money than they ever dreamed they would have. Where are they now? Many squandered their money on frivolous or luxury items only to find when the dot-com bubble burst that they were left no better off—and sometimes worse—than they were before they earned the money. Similarly, you hear of people who win the lottery and blow it on cars, trips, and houses they never really wanted. Before long, they're back at the jobs they quit when the windfall arrived.

You can't make up for lost time by spending money. What good does it do to buy all the things you thought could never belong to you, but not have time to spend with your family? Or to be so busy earning the money that you can't take a vacation? Living a rich life is about just that—*living*, not spending.

COACHING TIPS

- **Ask yourself whom you're trying to impress.** In the late nineteenth century Thorstein Veblen coined the term *conspicuous consumption* to describe the ostentatious spending by the wealthy class in an effort to advertise their wealth. If you're not from wealth, but have acquired it, you may find yourself buying things to show others you've "arrived." Whether it's showing your father, who always said you'd never amount to anything, or trying to impress the neighbors, buying things just because you can have them—not because you really need or want them—will only impede leading a rich life in the truest sense.

- **Return to your values.** If it's a rich life that you want, buying *things* won't get you there. As many Americans are finding, wealth can be illusory. It can disappear with one catastrophic illness or downturn in the economic climate. Live according to your values, not according to your paycheck.

- **Plan on how you will spend your inheritance.** Whether it comes as a surprise to you or you couldn't wait to get your hands on it, your inheritance is one of the last chances you will get to acquire wealth in large amounts. If you must be self-indulgent, take a small amount when you first receive it (I'm talking 5 percent, not 50 percent) and blow it on whatever you want. Once you've gotten this out of your system, think about how you can best invest the rest in your future.

Mistake 26

Not Distinguishing between Wants and Needs

*U*nity Marketing is a firm with the express mission of "helping companies unite with their target markets through consumer insight." In other words, they *find ways to get you to spend your money on things you don't really need*. A 2002 press release of theirs was titled "Desire, Not Necessity, Drives $3 Trillion in Consumer Spending." Pam Danzinger, president of Unity Marketing, expanded on this during a CNN interview when she claimed, "Consumers today spend proportionately less on basic necessities like food, clothing, shelter than they did twenty-five, thirty-five, even fifty years ago. But they spend more and more money on discretionary items that are motivated by emotion and desire."

Consider these top ten categories of things people buy that they don't really need:

1. Entertainment such as CDs, videotapes, and DVDs
2. Books and magazines
3. Greeting cards and personal stationery
4. Personal care products (beyond toothpaste and soap)
5. Candles
6. Home textiles such as pillows, rugs, and table linens
7. Seeds, plants, trees, shrubs, and other items used for landscaping
8. Kitchenware and accessories
9. Seasonal decorations
10. Toys, dolls, and games

What makes the list most interesting is that women are more likely than men to make the purchases in nine of the ten categories (items 2 through 10). Men do tend to buy big-ticket items, but the number of transactions are far fewer. Women tend to buy *what they want and when they want it*.

When you don't have much money, it's fairly easy to distinguish between what you need (money for rent, food, clothes for the kids) and what you want. Women on welfare are often better at budgeting and planning their spending than women with extra cash in their pockets. That cash can make a huge difference in the perception of what you can and can't afford. And that's a mistake.

How many times do you walk into a store to buy something you legitimately need only to walk out with five more things you supposedly can't live without? Those retailers really know how to get a girl where it hurts—especially ones that are using the research conducted by firms like Unity Marketing. That display with cashmere sweaters on sale is like a black hole. All logic that would help you to distinguish *needing* that sweater from *wanting* that sweater suddenly vanishes.

For women fortunate enough to have discretionary money (and for many who don't) it can be truly difficult to distinguish between a want and a need. We trick ourselves into believing we really need that extra pair of shoes because we have to look good at work if we want to get that promotion that will in turn lead to earning more money. When was the last time you got a promotion because you had two pairs of really expensive black shoes?

COACHING TIPS

- **Consciously consider wants versus needs.** When you're looking at an item you hadn't planned on purchasing, ask yourself what's more important: that you buy it or that you experience the freedom that comes from accumulating the amount of wealth you need to be truly free from the dictates of others.

- **Don't try it on.** There's some kind of voodoo that happens between the time you consider buying an item of clothing and the time you try it on. Taking it into the dressing room all but makes it yours. Before trying something on, ask yourself if you really need it. If the answer is no, put it down.

- **Avoid the mall altogether.** One study reports that only 25 percent of all visits to a mall or shopping center are for the express purpose of making an intentional purchase. The remaining visits are for recreational or entertainment purposes. Unless you have a particular purchase in mind, why not use that time to take a walk, visit with a friend, or take up a hobby?

- **Factor in your priorities.** There are times when you're going to buy something you don't need but really want. You know it will make you happy for a long time. Before making the purchase, though, consider your priorities in the moment. Have you recently changed jobs and are unsure about future income? Do you have an upcoming vacation? Is there dental work you have to have done? Get your priorities straight before making those emotional "gotta have it" purchases.

Mistake 27

Giving In to Social Pressure

*O*ne of the biggest mistakes I've made around money is allowing myself to be bullied into contributing to group gifts at an expense greater than I wanted to spend," said Ursula in response to the question of what behaviors have prevented her from becoming rich. Now, for most of us, it doesn't take much bullying to make us want to spend money. There are, however, times when social or peer pressure interferes with even our own limited best judgment about spending.

Social-pressure spending is different from guilt giving. Social pressure often causes us to spend more than we have or more than we want to. When it comes to gift giving, if everyone else is giving gifts in the $50-to-$100 range, you may feel as if you have to do the same. After all, you don't want to look cheap . . . do you? It's the opposite of the old maxim that it's not the cost but the thought that counts. Women know it had to be a man who made that one up!

I suffer from a unique form of social-pressure spending that some of you might relate to. My mother loved to shop, but she didn't like to spend money. As odd as that may sound, the fact is that she was a product of the Depression era, so she would buy only things that were on sale or that were in some other way bargains. I can recall her coming home from one of her shopping excursions with a gift for a friend or family member that she got on sale. It often didn't matter whether or not the person would like it or that it was picked out exclusively with that person in mind—it was such a good deal and *she* liked it. Then for the next several hours she would ask me a dozen times, "Do you think it looks too cheap?" What I wanted to say was, "If you thought it looked too cheap, why did you buy it?" But instead, it only served to bolster the resolve in me never to buy a gift that might "look cheap," because I didn't want to have to worry like my mother did. I actually suffered from the same fear my mother did—but expressed it in the opposite way in order to ward off potential social criticism.

Another form of social pressure is the need to keep up "appearances" or keep up with the Joneses. This can translate into buying a more expensive car than you can afford, blowing an entire month's clothing budget on one pair of designer shoes because everyone else is wearing them, or going to the most expensive restaurant in town because that's where a friend wanted to go. Anytime you spend more money than you think is prudent because it's expected or because you can't say no, you've succumbed to social pressure.

COACHING TIPS

• **Stick to your budget.** A little later I'll be talking about budgets, but social pressure is another good reason why you should have one. By sitting down at the beginning of the year and making a list of discretionary spending (gifts, dinners out, family vacations, etc.), you're circumscribing the boundaries within which you should be spending. Of course, there will always be exceptions as you go through the year, but your budget—not social pressure—will dictate how much money you can afford to spend on each gift, dinner, or trip throughout the year.

• **Select gifts with the person in mind.** You are much less likely to succumb to social-pressure spending if you set out to purchase a gift with a certain person in mind. Doing so allows you to select something you know the person will actually like, not something you think looks expensive. Another suggestion when it comes to gift giving is to ask people what they would like as a gift. Most people are likely to suggest something that fits your budget, and you can be more confident that it is something they would actually like to receive.

• **Host group activities where everyone participates.** For example, rather than go to an expensive restaurant, have a potluck where everyone brings something. Organize a beach barbecue rather than spend more than you can afford on a luxury hotel. Or have a white elephant gift exchange. With so many people getting into the phenomenon recently named "regifting" (giving someone a gift you received that you don't want or don't like), this can be a free and fun way to exchange gifts with an entire group of people. Just be careful not to bring something to exchange that has been given to you by someone attending the event.

Mistake 28

First-Job Syndrome

*Y*oung women fresh out of school with their first paychecks are particularly likely to succumb to this mistake. Despite the fact that many of them have parents who taught them the importance of saving—for either the future or a rainy day—what's left over after paying for the monthly essentials burns a hole in their pockets. It's seen as "free money." So what do they do? Spend it!

When you're twenty-two years old, it can be hard to picture yourself as an eighty-year-old living on a fixed income. If more of us did, we'd have much larger portfolios. It's important to factor into your thinking that discretionary income is *not* what's left over after you pay your bills; it's what's left over after you've paid the bills *and* funded your retirement account or savings plan. Investing and saving for retirement are not optional, they're essential. Don't delude yourself into thinking your employer, family, or Social Security will take care of your expenses when you retire or that what's left over once you pay the bills is yours to spend freely. It's your responsibility to secure your financial future—and that responsibility begins as soon as you start working.

Still finding it difficult to imagine yourself as an eighty-year-old retiree? Try picturing yourself as a twenty-six-year-old with a maxed-out Visa, car payment, and rent who just got caught in the company's downsizing. What's that sound you hear? Oh, it's your muffler, overflowing toilet, broken garbage disposal, or eyeglasses that you just stepped on. Get the picture? A first job means it's your first opportunity to create an emergency fund. This is one habit that will literally save you again and again for the rest of your life.

COACHING TIPS

• **Plan your "mad money."** Give yourself permission to take a portion (a small portion) of what's left over from your paycheck, after you've paid your bills, to use as "mad money." You can spend this on anything you like, but once it's gone, there's no going back to the money wall (the ATM). Similarly, if there's nothing you particularly want, carry it over to the next month.

• **Make it a habit to save a percentage of every paycheck.** A friend of mine who retired by age fifty called this "paying yourself first." You don't have to deprive yourself (although you might be able to live with a little less) but do get into the habit of saving. It's just that: a habit. And like every other good habit, it takes work to make it stick. Consider it building your financial muscle.

Mistake 29

Spending Money to Save Money

$\mathcal{I}$n my household we have a joke: We can't shop at the warehouse clubs because we can't afford to save so much money. Don't get me wrong—you can legitimately find great deals on many items at these clubs, but anyone who buys in bulk at these discount warehouses knows what I'm talking about. You buy six giant-size boxes of cereal bound together because you save 25 percent over buying individual boxes at the grocery store. Of course, you often wind up throwing half of the boxes out because they go stale before you can use them. Or you have an entire linen closet filled with toilet paper—something that will never go bad, so why not? London broil for just seventy-nine cents per pound? I'd better get three and freeze them. Of course, I forget they're in there until I'm looking for something to make for dinner and find them with freezer burn and totally inedible. One woman told me her mother took one of the rooms in her house, formerly a child's bedroom, and now uses it as a storage room. "She can supply the entire city of Cleveland with paper towels for a year," she groaned.

Then there's sale shopping. Go count how many pieces of apparel you have in your closet that still have the tags on and that you'll probably donate to Goodwill before you ever wear them. But such a deal! A study of 529 Iowa residents found that women were nearly *five times* more likely than men to buy something because it was on sale and twice as likely to buy things they don't need. Compound that with buying on credit that you don't pay off in full each month instead of paying with cash, and the net savings from the sale becomes moot.

What's wrong with having a closet full of clothes you don't wear or need and extra boxes of cereal, toilet paper, or paper towels? Aside from the fact that some items do spoil before you can use them, it's the same as having money sit in your closet earning no interest and accumulating no value. You are literally throwing your money away! Had you just gone to the store and bought one box of cereal at twice the price, one London broil at full price, or a blouse at retail, you would be left with money to invest. Don't kid yourself—those little purchases add up.

COACHING TIPS

• **Determine the real cost of buying in bulk or buying sale items.** Bulk buying is not the best deal for everyone. If you live alone or with only one or two other people, the potential savings on comestibles goes down the drain with spoilage, and in turn the price of what you actually used goes up. If you buy two cartons of milk on sale and wind up throwing one out because it goes bad before you can use it, you've probably paid at least one and a half times the value of what you actually consumed. The same holds true for clothing and other household items you buy on sale—you're not saving money if you don't use them.

• **Credit cards—you *can* leave home without them.** When you take that charge card out for purchases, it doesn't hurt quite so much as when you lay down cold, hard cash. We've gotten used to keeping little cash in our wallets and as a result spend more now than ever. Get in the habit of taking a fixed amount of cash with you when you shop and leave the credit cards at home.

• **Keep track of discretionary spending.** Even if you aren't disciplined enough to keep a written record of discretionary spending, there's another way to accomplish the same end. Save every receipt, ticket stub, credit slip, and ATM receipt in your wallet for one month. As you watch your wallet begin to bulge, let it serve as a reminder of just how much you're spending. Make a game out of seeing how long it takes you to reduce that bulge from month to month. Pretty soon you'll start questioning how much you really need that item—even if it's only a five-dollar tube of lipstick.

• **Toss out sale flyers.** It's better not to know how much you could save at that Macy's twelve-hour sale, Nordstrom's twice-a-year sale, or Talbot's summer sale.

Mistake 30

Not Taking Time to Research

*A*s busy as we all are these days with taking care of everyone else's needs, it's no wonder women don't take the time to research before buying. But not making the time to figure out where you can get the best price on that laptop you need, the best pricing plan for your cellular phone, or the gift you want to give to your brother for his birthday winds up costing you hundreds—if not thousands—of extra dollars every year. In "the olden days" we used to have to go from store to store in an effort to find out who had the best prices. Now all you have to do is sit down at your computer and search the Internet—and we often *still* don't do it!

Whether you're buying a car or a computer, you shouldn't be laying down any of your hard-earned money before you know whether or not you're getting the best price. It's not only the Internet that can help you—ask friends or family members if they've seen or heard of any sales related to the item you're interested in purchasing. My cousin recently wanted to buy a digital camcorder for her husband for Father's Day. She happened to mention it one day during a conversation, and I happened to have just bought one for our office. I'd already done all the research on different kinds and different prices (using the Internet) and was able to direct her to a store near her office in Manhattan where she saved nearly $100 over one she had seen elsewhere. What would *you* do with an extra $100 in savings?

COACHING TIPS

- **Check out Web sites that allow you to compare prices.**
There are several sites that provide excellent information as
a place to start—even if you want to make the actual purchase locally. Several to consider are:

    www.mysimon.com

    www.nextag.com

    www.bizrate.com

    www.pricescan.com

    www.shrewd.com

- **Subscribe to *Consumer Reports*.** It contains not only
price comparisons but also testing of everything from auto-
mobiles to washing machines. You'll make up the cost of the
subscription in no time.

- **Wait for a sale.** With few exceptions, sooner or later
almost every item in any store is discounted. You can count
on there being an annual white sale, deep discounts on cars
when the new models arrive, and end-of-season sales on out-
door items. I had my eye on a patio table and decided to wait
until late summer to see if it would be marked down. Sure
enough, I went to the store and it was discounted by 20 percent. It's not that I couldn't afford to buy it at full price—but
why do so when I can use the savings on something else?

- **Take advantage of "no payments, no interest" offers.** If
you're going to buy a big-ticket item such as a mattress, appli-
ance, or television, this can be a good deal *provided* you pay it
off in full when the first bill arrives. They're banking on the
likelihood that you won't pay it off in one lump sum and they
will earn money on the interest you then pay. Keeping the
money you would have spent up front on the item in your savings account earning interest is a smart way to use the store's
money to make money for you.

- **Read the rater reviews of online retailers.** Many of the comparison sites have ratings from actual users of the retailers they list. These are particularly helpful when you are trying to determine whether you want to buy the item online or locally.

- **Negotiate.** If you find a good price on the Internet but want to buy locally, print out the page where you found it and bring it to your local retailer. It doesn't always help, but it never hurts.

- **Beware of refurbished goods.** If a price seems absolutely too good to be true, it may be just that. Particularly with electronics, Internet sellers will often indicate in the fine print that this is a refurbished item. These aren't always bad deals, but you've got to decide in advance if you're willing to take the risk of aggravation down the road in exchange for saving money.

Mistake 31

Ignoring Rebates, Cash Back, and Mileage Options

 *F*or nearly twenty years I have been registered with United Airlines for Mileage Plus Rewards. You may know how these programs work but have never taken the time to sign up. It costs nothing to enroll, and you receive a bonus mile for each mile you fly with an airline or one of the airline's partners. Points can then be redeemed for travel. I've vacationed in England, New Zealand, France (several times), Italy, Hawaii, Spain, and Peru—for free. All because I take time to keep track of my account and make a point of flying with United or one of its partner airlines.

Similar deals are available with other airlines, various credit card companies, and some retailers. Kathleen Booth, an executive with Warner Bros., turned me on to several new Web sites that offer savings in the form of the return of a small percentage of the purchase price of an item for particular retailers. For example, BondRewards.com represents merchandisers such as Macy's, Avon, RadioShack, Baby Gap, and more. When you register for a bond account with them and shop online with one of their retailers, they put a percentage of your purchases (ranging from 1 to 10 percent) into your account. This amount can then be redeemed for savings bonds or merchandise.

Another Web site, Nesteggz.com, allows you to have rebates sent to you via check or deposited directly into your retirement savings account. The service is free, and you can direct this money into virtually any retirement savings vehicle you choose, except a 401(k) plan. The requirement here is that when you shop in-store or dine at restaurants represented by Nesteggz, you have to use their credit card to pay for your merchandise or services. Not a bad deal if you're the type who pays off all credit card balances each month. And this is a big caveat: Buying things you really don't need just for the sake of getting rebates will never get you rich.

COACHING TIPS

• **Take time to complete rebate forms.** Many stores lure you in with advertisements for rock-bottom prices on big-ticket items, but when you get there, you find out the price requires you to send in for a rebate. They're betting that you won't take the time to complete the paperwork required to receive the rebate. Even though the forms and documentation are annoying, it really can save you hundreds of dollars during the course of a year, depending on the size of your purchases.

• **Choose credit cards with no or low annual fees plus incentives.** In addition to being a member of the Mileage Plus Rewards program, I use my United Airlines Visa card for all my business purchases. For each dollar I spend using the card (even for airline tickets) I receive another mile in my travel account. Even though there's an annual fee, the amount of miles I accrue over the year more than covers it. Weigh the amount you spend each year on credit cards against the annual fee to see if a particular card is worth it to you.

• **Check out online incentive programs.** Some are free, others charge a nominal fee for enrollment—which may or may not be worth it depending on your spending habits. A few for you to consider are listed in chapter 9.

Mistake 32

Not Selecting the Right Automobile Financing Option

*S*hould you lease or buy a car? Plenty of women wind up buying a car when they would be better off leasing, and, conversely, plenty lease a car when it would be more financially prudent for them to buy it. Al Jennings, director of Western Fleet Auto Brokers, has been an independent car broker for almost forty years. During this time he has seen people make mistakes that ended up costing them thousands of dollars. "No one should sign a vehicle lease if they do not totally understand what they're doing," says Jennings. Although leasing can provide tax advantages for certain people, far too many people lease when they would be better off purchasing.

Leasing a vehicle differs from buying in that an actual purchase allows you to pay for the entire vehicle over a period of time, at the end of which you own the car. With a lease, you pay only the amount the vehicle is projected to depreciate while you have it, and at the end of the lease period you turn in the car. Leasing is sometimes a good idea, but it has many hidden pitfalls. Here are some of the potential pitfalls Jennings urges you to consider before leasing your next car:

- Many dealers advertise a very low payment on a car lease, which in turn requires a large down payment. The problem with this is that the large down payment is gone at the end of the lease—and so is the car. This leaves you with nothing to "trade up with" for your next vehicle.
- Lease interest rates are not disclosed on the contract, and very high rates can be well concealed by a greedy dealer.

No matter how low your payments are, paying too much interest is never in your best interests.

- When quoted at all, lease "interest" is shown as a lease "factor," not an APR (annual percentage rate). People mistakenly think a 2.5 percent lease factor is 2.5 percent APR when, in fact, you multiply the lease factor by 2,400 to get the real APR. So, for example, a 2.5 percent lease factor is actually a 6 percent APR. If you could have gotten a lower rate buying the car, then you lost money on the lease interest, no matter how low the payment is.

- Many leases are computed on a 10,000- or 12,000-mile-per-year basis. This is fine if that is realistically all you are going to drive. But the fact is that most people drive more than that, and the penalty for high mileage is usually fifteen to twenty cents per mile over the allocated mileage. Disreputable salespeople often promise to get you out of a lease when you go over your allocated mileage, but in reality they plan to overcharge you for the *next* vehicle you lease to "bury" your overmileage penalty. Again, the next car ends up costing more than it should, or you have to pay a significant amount of money to get out of the first lease.

- Leases have hidden charges, typically several hundred dollars in "acquisition fees" added to the front end as well as fees added at the termination of the lease. The combination can be $1,000 or more.

- Many people are best off keeping a vehicle for most of its useful life, which would typically be seven to ten years. Most leases have a three- or four-year term, forcing the lessee to "purchase" roughly twice as many vehicles as they would if they bought the car. Only a rare few vehicles depreciate less annually in their first four years than they do over a longer period.

Don't let these pitfalls scare you away from leasing a car, because there are advantages—particularly if you're a business owner or are self-employed. The primary benefits to you if you fall into either of these categories are that (1) leasing a car allows you to write off a high percentage of the lease amount as an operating expense against your business income, (2) not putting a large down payment on a car leaves you with more cash flow that may be more advantageous to you than having that money tied up in a car, and (3) because leased cars are typically traded every two or three years, maintenance costs are often less than they are with older vehicles. Even if you're not a business owner or self-employed, you may find yourself needing a new car at a time when you can least afford it and the lease option allows you to get into a car with far less money down than if you purchase it. If you want to determine whether leasing is really a good deal for you, consider the following coaching tips provided by Jennings.

COACHING TIPS

• **Don't make car financing decisions based solely on a monthly payment.** A car depreciates the same whether you lease it or buy it. If the combination of your cash down payment and monthly payments doesn't keep up with depreciation, the "moment of truth" will come at the end of the lease if you decide to buy the same vehicle. If you can't afford a realistic payment on a car, you can't afford the car. Choose something you *can* afford without any creative financing. No matter how exciting the car is, you will grow to hate it if you are "upside down" in it for too long.

• **Consider leasing if the following circumstances apply to you:**

- You completely understand the lease contract, the hidden charges, the interest rate, and the lease-end charges, and you realistically estimate the actual mileage and wear and tear the vehicle will sustain.
- You would normally trade cars as often as the lease calls for. That is, you're the kind of person who wants a new car every two or three years.
- You need a new car and you don't have the down payment required to buy it.
- You will drive the car no more miles than the lease allows you to (typically 10,000 to 12,000 miles).
- You can make a minimum down payment (first payment and license fees only) and still afford the monthly payment.
- You are signing a true closed-end lease in which the lessor (not you) is responsible for guaranteeing the buyout value (residual) at the end of the lease. The residual value of the car (the amount you would pay if you purchased it at the end of the lease) is often $3,000 to $4,000 more than the actual value of the car at that point.
- You have "slept" on the deal overnight, figured the total actual cost, and it is no more than buying the same vehicle.

- **Do your homework.** Whether you decide to buy or lease a car, shop around to make sure you're getting the best deal. As with any purchase, be sure you have a dollar amount in mind that you're willing to spend so that you don't exceed your budget. And if you're not a particularly good negotiator, try using a car broker or Internet car buying service. The Web site www.leaseguide.com has more information on the differences between buying and leasing a car and a calculator to help you determine the difference in the costs.

Chapter Five

Learning Money Basics

Don't marry for money. You can borrow it cheaper.

It doesn't matter if you earn $2,000 a month or $20,000. You need to keep track of how you are using and losing your money. If doing this seems like more trouble than it's worth, think again. I'm not just talking about budgeting and balancing your checkbook—I'm also talking about knowing how your investments are growing or losing their value. Women have shared horror stories about turning entire portfolios over to their husbands (just ask Barbara Stanny), family members, or other financial professionals to manage for them, only to one day learn these so-called money managers have lost their entire fortunes.

Getting rich isn't just about accumulating money and assets, it's about managing them too. It does no good to buy a house, then not maintain it. If you don't service your car, you risk running it into the ground. You wouldn't think of throwing that $200 cashmere sweater into the washer. These are all assets you attend to and take care of—just as you should focus on taking care of your money.

The tips found in this chapter are designed to help you get into the habit of attending to your money as well as you attend to matters such as your hair, clothing, and home decor. Tracking your money can take as little as an hour a month. In fact, the simpler you keep it, the better. You're more likely to do it if it's not a cumbersome and complex process. It's about being more conscious of where your money is going and how it's growing and having the systems in place to help you with the process.

Mistake 33

Not Budgeting

*L*et me get this one over with right up front. I hate budgets. For that matter, I hate anything conforming, controlling, or confining. I don't like to know how much money I shouldn't be spending any more than I like being told I can't eat carbohydrates. With that said, you *can* budget and plan without feeling deprived. Financial experts will tell you that you should have a monthly budget and adhere to it fairly rigidly. It's not that they're wrong—it's just that if you're anything like me, you're never going to do it.

You'll never get rich if you're one of those women who think they can spend money as long as they have checks in their checkbook or "available credit" on their charge cards. A budget shouldn't feel restrictive to you. If anything, it should free you up to spend without guilt because you know how much you have available to spend. Look at a budget as nothing more than a plan that will make you more *conscious* of how you spend your money.

Interestingly, one of the mistakes some women shared with us was regret over *not* spending more money on themselves or on the things that would bring them joy. "The most foolish thing I've done related to money was spend too much of my life worrying about whether I had enough or didn't have enough," said one such woman. "I always felt I never had enough. I cheated myself out of living in the moment, and I'll bet I die with a lot left over." If she only had a budget. Consider a budget your guide for living a more—not less—abundant life.

COACHING TIPS

• **Do your bill paying with Microsoft Money or Quicken.** These inexpensive and easy-to-use software programs let you get rid of your checkbook and keep it all in one file on your desktop or laptop. You can either print or still write out your checks, but the tracking is done for you. With the push of a button you can see at a glance where your money is going. If you're really good with computers, you can create charts and graphs that reflect your expenditures. I even find it kind of fun, and as you already know—I hate budgets.

• **Consider what the experts say about where your money should be going.** On the next page there's a table that shows recommendations for monthly expenditures. Take a minute now to compare your spending with these suggestions. Mark the page and come back to it when you have more time to see where you could benefit from shifting some of your money from one category to another. You might even find that you can afford to buy a house, new car, or other item you've been depriving yourself of because you weren't sure you could afford it.

TYPICAL MONTHLY EXPENSES

EXPENDITURE	% OF BUDGET*	YOUR SPENDING
Savings/investing	10+	
Mortgage/rent	25–40	
Home-related expense	8–15	
Food	10–20	
Car/transportation	15–25	
Medical	8–15	
Clothing	3–5	
Personal/ miscellaneous	5–10	
Personal debt (student loans, personal loans, etc.)	Under 5	

* Note that because these are ranges, the percentage of the budget column does not add up to 100 percent. Since everyone's finances are different, you might be able to put more into one area and less into another. *Your* budget, however, must total 100 percent of your income.

Mistake 34

Paying Bills, Not Managing Money

*W*omen are often the ones in a household who assume the task of paying the monthly bills. This is obviously true if you're single, but married or partnered women frequently find themselves in the role of writing out the checks. The irony is that many never make the leap from paying the bills to managing their money or being involved in the management of the family's wealth. Well, if you can pay bills, you can manage money in the broadest sense.

Paying the household bills puts you in the perfect position to understand and participate in the family's investment strategies. Who knows better than you what you have coming in and going out? Single or partnered, the problem is that you may be doing the chore routinely rather than looking at the bigger picture. Managing the household finances is more than simply making sure your creditors get their money on time. It's about ensuring that you and your family are financially secure. It's the difference between buying the groceries and making the meal. One is a task; the other requires skill, creativity, and execution.

In a meeting I had with several women investment advisers and CPAs, I was told a story about a woman who had total responsibility for managing the day-to-day household finances but was asked to leave the room when investment strategies were discussed. My jaw dropped. I asked if this happened in 2004 or decades before. I was assured that this happened in the recent past and continues to happen in many households. What surprised me even more than the fact that the woman was asked to leave the room was that she complied! Talk about being a "nice girl"!

COACHING TIPS

• **Don't be a functionary; be a partner in the financial planning process.** Talk to your spouse or partner about his/her investment strategies. Inform him that you want to be included in discussions, meetings, and decisions related to investments. Offer to schedule the meetings at a time convenient for you both. Don't assume because you're not currently included it means you're not welcome. It could just be that your partner assumes you don't want to be involved if you've never before expressed an interest.

• **Read the financial statements that come in the mail or online.** Don't just put that mail aside to read later (which, if you're like me, you might prefer to do) or for your partner to read. Use a portion of your "get rich" time to sit down and understand your investments. You don't have to overanalyze them. Something simple that I do each month when the statements arrive is look at the bottom line for a month-to-month comparison. Do I have more money in my accounts than I did the month before? If not, why not? It could be that the markets took a dive the past month, in which case I may or may not speak with my financial adviser about whether I should do something about it. It could also be that someone withdrew money from the investments or that there's an error. In any case, you won't know if you don't look.

• **Dare to be assertive.** The truth of the matter is that many spouses would just as soon keep you ignorant about the family's finances. Money isn't only an emotionally laden topic for women—it can be for men too. Particularly men who aren't doing such a great job of managing the family's port-folio! If it's suggested that you don't need to "worry your pretty little head" about money (or in so many words), affirmatively state that you're not worried about it, that you're interested in learning and knowing where the family money is going.

Mistake 35

Not Balancing Your Checkbook

*H*ow many of us have joked that as long as there are checks in the checkbook, we figure we have money to spend? It wasn't so funny for this woman who shared this story with us:

> When I first moved to California, I deposited a rather large sum of money in my checking account. Shortly thereafter I made out my tuition check for the graduate school I was attending. The only problem was that I added the sum instead of deducting it when I wrote the check. Because there was plenty of money in the account and because I don't balance my checkbook, it took a couple of months to catch up with me. Then suddenly, I was bouncing checks all over town! By the way, at the time I was studying mathematics at Stanford University.

You may wonder how not balancing your checkbook impedes your ability to get rich. As this woman found out, bouncing checks is one surefire way to put a stain on your credit rating. Balancing your checkbook is just another way to ensure you stay on top of and in control of your finances. If you're one of those people who make deposits but don't reconcile their checkbook, then you're more likely to treat money as dispensable—not something that has to be cared for and looked after. It's the attitude around money that impedes the ability to get rich, not the act of balancing the checkbook itself.

COACHING TIPS

- **Switch to online banking.** Personally, I have found it much easier to reconcile my accounts since I switched from manually writing checks and balancing the checkbooks. You have a flawless record of what actually went out and an up-to-date method of seeing what's in the account—and it doesn't make errors of addition and subtraction! Being busy or out of town when your monthly statement comes is often an excuse for not balancing your account at all. The online banking system allows you to reconcile your accounts at your convenience, not when the statements arrive.

- **Make a calendar notation to review your online accounts twice per month.** Again, online banking has made it easy for you to pull up your account and get the latest information about what's in the account and what's not. It's more likely that you'll remember your transactions, so if a mistake is made, you can recall where it could have occurred. Calendaring it makes it a formal "appointment" that you make with yourself to actually take the time to do it.

- **Don't just balance, *analyze* your account.** Accounting software like Microsoft Money (which often comes with your operating system) has become so easy to use there's no reason why you should still be doing everything manually. It also allows you to look at where your money is going. When setting up your electronic account, categorize your expenditures so that you can see at a glance how much is going into household expenses like rent or mortgage, utilities, and housekeeping. Also have discretionary categories such as meals out, clothing, and gifts so you can see how you're using the rest of your money.

- **Watch your ATM transactions.** One friend's grandchild calls the ATM "the money wall." And the money wall is dangerous. It allows you to take out small amounts each time that add up to large amounts over time. Instead of making multiple trips to the ATM, figure out how much you need each week for pocket money, withdraw it on Sunday or Monday, and live within your budget.

Mistake 36

Ignoring Monthly Statements

*H*ow many times have you closed a checking account because you waited so long to balance it that the task became utterly impossible? Or are you one of those people that round your checking account up each time you write a check just to make sure you always have enough in it? During the most recent economic decline did you ignore monthly portfolio statements only to realize one day that your investments had lost a significant amount of their value? If you answered yes to any of these questions, join the club—the I'm Never Going to Be Rich Club, that is. These are real examples shared with us by real women.

Not attending to your finances is much like blindly entrusting your money to others—which in many ways is precisely what you are doing. Whether it's trusting the bank to accurately record a deposit, or a mutual fund manager to pick your stocks, when you don't regularly review your assets, you can set yourself up for a surprise. This is exactly what happened to Carmen, the owner of a small boutique in New England. Overwhelmed with running a business and a single-parent household, she would make deposits and write checks every month without ever taking time to reconcile her bank account. Suddenly, she was bouncing payroll checks and payments to creditors. She knew business was slower than usual, but she also knew she wasn't spending more than she made.

When Carmen sat down with the books to try to figure out what was happening, it was impossible. She was able to track back about six months, but records beyond that were either lost or indecipherable. She finally brought in an accountant, who found that eighteen months previously she had made a substantial deposit that appeared not to have been recorded by the bank. Because her cash flow situation had been so good for so long, the missing money wasn't noticed. Once the cash flow slowed down, however, the missing money made a difference. The only problem was, because she had waited so long, she couldn't prove the bank had made a mistake and she was out nearly $15,000 plus the cost of the professional accounting services.

If women didn't have to make dinner, clean the house, pick up the kids, service their own cars, take care of elderly parents, *and* work a job outside the home, I wonder if they would pay closer attention to their finances. I would like to think so, but in my heart of hearts I would have to say that not many women would use the time to track where their money is going and how it's growing (or declining). That's why the following coaching tips are so important!

COACHING TIPS

• **At a minimum scan your account statements.** Check out the total deposits and total withdrawals on your checking account statement. With portfolio statements check to see that dividends have been reinvested and that there are no withdrawals you didn't authorize. Also check the difference in the beginning and ending balance. Glaring errors can usually be revealed by even a cursory review. Keep in mind that "buy and hold" investments don't mean "buy, hold, and ignore."

• **Schedule a yearly tune-up with a financial adviser.** If you don't want to pay for the services of an adviser on a regular basis, it's still worth the time and money at least once a year to sit down with a financial professional who can help you decipher the progress you've made with your investments. At the risk of alienating some friends and colleagues, I advise that you avoid the big investment firms for this kind of annual review even if their services are free, because eventually they'll gain from your investments with them. Instead, choose an independent adviser who charges by the hour.

Mistake 37

Signing Tax Returns without Reviewing Them

$\mathcal{M}$argo owns a small hair salon in Phoenix. She was separated, but not divorced, from her husband, who always prepared their joint tax returns. Each year he would appear at the shop on April 14 and rush her through signing the returns so that he could make the deadline for mailing them. One day she received a letter from the IRS claiming they owed nearly $50,000 in back taxes, penalties, and interest. Certainly, it was a mistake, she thought. She confronted her estranged husband, and after he hemmed and hawed, she asked for a copy of their returns for the past five years. He didn't want to give them to her, but ultimately relented when Margo's attorney called and demanded he turn them over.

Margo then had an independent certified public accountant review the returns. Sure enough, her husband had grossly underreported their combined earned incomes, neglected to report other sources of income, and misrepresented the amount of loss on stock sales. To make matters worse, the previous year he had filed for bankruptcy and claimed he had no assets from which to pay the IRS. The result: Since she was still legally married to this man, Margo was responsible for paying all of what was owed to the government.

How many times have you been handed a set of completed tax returns and signed your name to them without looking them over? If someone other than you prepares the returns, it's a huge mistake to simply affix your signature and mail them. You are financially responsible for any and all errors contained on a tax return—whether those errors are made intentionally or accidentally.

COACHING TIPS

• **Check the basics.** You don't have to be a tax expert to review your tax returns before affixing your signature. Elaine Gregory, a partner in the accounting firm Gregory, Filas Associates in Pasadena, California, suggests some basic things to review before signing the return:

- If the adjusted gross income on your tax return reports very little income yet you, or you and your family, are living quite well, ask the preparer how this can be. It could be an honest mistake, or it could be that income is being underreported.
- Read pages 1 and 2 of the return to see if the bottom line makes sense to you.
- Look at schedule A, itemized deductions. If you notice that there are large amounts listed for contributions you don't remember making or losses you don't think were incurred, don't hesitate to ask how the number was arrived at.
- Check the income from interest and ordinary dividends on schedule B. Again, these should pass the "commonsense" test for you.
- If you or your spouse own a business, check schedules C (net profit from business) and E (supplemental income or loss) for other forms of income and losses from partnerships.

Mistake 38

Ignoring What You Don't Spend

*A*s I've said before, being rich isn't just about having money in the bank. It's about having and doing the things you most enjoy in life and still being financially independent. One of the women we surveyed, when asked about the most foolish mistakes she's made with money, told us, "Never learning to enjoy the money I accumulated. Giving it too much power and always worrying about not having enough." You can't take it with you, so give yourself credit for a job well done. Reward yourself when you reach financial benchmarks.

COACHING TIPS

• **Create a personal credit account.** One of the fun things you can do while tracking your finances is to keep a log of the money you save when you don't make that impulse purchase or when you've successfully researched how to get the best price on a necessity. Keep a running tally of your total savings.

• **Shift savings to investments.** If you saved $3,000 to purchase a new computer, and through careful research and comparison shopping you found exactly what you wanted for $2,500, invest the difference. Since you weren't planning on having that money anyway, and you did get what you wanted, immediately put that money to work for you.

• **Treat yourself with a percentage of the money you save from not spending.** Let's say you were *really* good. Among other things, you passed up that second pair of shoes at a Nordstrom sale, bought a fully equipped Toyota Avalon instead of the more expensive Lexus, and cooked at home rather than ordering takeout or making a weekly visit to your favorite restaurant. All told, in the past six months you saved $6,500. Celebrate your success. You can invest $6,000 of those savings and still treat yourself to a $500 guilt-free shopping spree.

Chapter Six

Saving and Investing for Future Wealth

And the trouble is, if you don't risk anything, you risk even more.

ERICA JONG

If there's one common financial regret among women once they reach midlife, it's that they didn't start saving early enough. As with all the mistakes in this book, the reasons vary from woman to woman but include thinking someone else will ultimately take care of them, living in the moment and not thinking about the future, and being uninterested in money managing. Regardless of your age, there's nothing more important than to begin or continue to accumulate and grow your wealth. But if you're a young woman just starting out, take heed of this particular regret of your older sisters.

Similarly, it doesn't matter if you're in a high or low income bracket. Women in both categories find excuses for not saving and investing in the future. Whereas a woman in a higher income bracket should theoretically have more money to save, she may mistakenly use most of her income to create a lifestyle rather than save. Buying those morning lattes, extra outfits, and expensive dinners with friends adds up to having less in your retirement and savings accounts than you could and should.

Conversely, saving and investing can be particularly difficult for women in lower income brackets. These women earn less and are more likely to pay for many of the expenses related to child rearing (clothing, school supplies, gifts, etc.), thereby leaving them with less money to save. But this can't be used as an excuse either. If you're barely making ends meet now, it's imperative that you use the tips in this book to create a plan for not only surviving but thriving. And that means planning your financial future, not just living in the present. We've all heard the stories about women who worked their entire lives in low-paying jobs yet accumulated enough to leave substantial bequests to colleges or charitable organizations.

It's not the actual amount of money that you earn that determines whether or not you'll be rich, it's what you *do* with what you earn. It's not even about having a lot of money to save, because every bit saved compounds into larger and larger amounts of money. That's where the saying "A penny saved is a penny earned" comes from. Saving and investing are crucial to creating enough wealth to live the life you want. Just because you're earning enough money now to afford to buy all those little niceties doesn't mean you'll be earning it next month or next year. Very few of us can predict what the future will bring, but saving and investing can ensure we live the life we want in the future. Let's take a look at what you're doing with your money.

Mistake 39

Not Having Investments in Your Name

*H*ave you ever wondered why more men than women urge their partners to put property or other investments in their name and their name alone? Worse yet, when you think like a "girl," you blindly go along with it. At the time of the request you might think, *Why not? I love and trust this person.* You might just find it easier to comply than to make waves. Or you might be relieved that someone else is willing to handle all of these affairs for you. The fact is, there is no good reason to put joint monies or property into one partner's name. Doing so leaves one person open to all the gain—or liability—associated with the investment.

Rita's case is particularly disturbing because it involves not only the loss of a loved one but deceit. Rita was married to Al for nearly six years when he suggested that all of their assets be transferred into his name so that he could more easily manage them. Her job had her traveling a lot, and Al, who was serially unemployed, found it cumbersome to get her signature and approval for the financial transactions he was undertaking. Although she had always been the bigger breadwinner in the family and contributed significantly more to their joint pot, she willingly went along. After all, she trusted him, she loved him, and she believed he had the best interests of her and their two young children at heart. In some convoluted way his request made sense to her.

As they approached their eighth year of marriage, Al decided he wanted a divorce. Rita claims she didn't see it coming. She thought they were happy together, and they rarely fought, experiencing only the normal ups and downs of any marriage. In her opinion there wasn't anything they couldn't work out. Yet Al pursued the divorce. Once Rita got over the emotional shock of being on her own with two children, she moved on to sorting out the divorce details. What she found was that other than child custody issues, there wasn't much to work out. She had no assets in her name, and Al had no intention of being fair. He used the fact that she had no money and no home in her name as a bargaining chip to get custody of the kids.

In another case Harriet was a young bride when she and her husband purchased a duplex. Her husband insisted on putting the property in his mother's name for tax purposes. Being naive and trusting, Harriet agreed. Over the next few years they continued to acquire income property. Harriet worked as a nurse, and her husband managed their real estate and other investments. Each time they bought a house or apartment, it went into his mother's name. I'm sure you can guess the end of the story. They divorced, and because very little of their joint savings and none of their property was in Harriet's name, she wound up with half of almost nothing and he wound up with all of the real estate holdings.

Situations such as these aren't as uncommon as you might think. "Nice girls" want to believe that their Prince Charming will take care of them, but as Barbara Stanny found out, *Prince Charming isn't coming*. I've said it before, I'll say it again, and you'll probably hear it yet again: *No one can take better care of you than you yourself*.

COACHING TIPS

• **Have a bank account and credit card in your own name.** Borrowing from the Virginia Woolf classic "A Room of One's

Own," every woman should have money that is hers alone. More and more couples are going this route. It doesn't mean you should put every penny you make into your own account or that all investments should be individual ones. It means there is no good reason for not having at least one account and one credit card that are yours alone in addition to a joint one to pay the household expenses. Not only is it financially prudent, it allows you to establish credit under your own name in the event you one day need it.

• **Never allow joint investments or property to be held under anything other than both names.** Even if your partner gives you a hundred good reasons why it should be held differently, the risks far outweigh any potential advantage should there be a death or divorce.

• **When relationships go south, don't negotiate alone.** No matter how amicable a divorce might seem, if there are any questions at all about joint property, you should consult a good lawyer or mediator. The emotions that are often present at times like this impede your ability to be a good advocate for yourself. Don't even try.

Mistake 40

Mismanaging Acquired Wealth

*H*orsemouth.com, a performance improvement network for financial advisers, estimates that over the next thirty years women will be the primary recipients of between $42 and $100 *trillion* of inherited wealth. That's the largest transfer of wealth in history. It doesn't matter if you inherit $500 or $5 million or if you receive half of the family assets in a divorce. It's *your* money and it's money that should be invested wisely. There are a number of ways in which women mismanage acquired wealth:

• Putting inherited money into a joint account
• Giving away large, unplanned amounts to charitable causes
• Making "loans" to friends and family members
• Easing the pain of your loss (either death or divorce) by spending large amounts of money

The financial advisers I spoke with told horror stories about women who blew fortunes on frivolous purchases, buying homes that were well beyond their means in the long term, and children who came to see them as the Bank of Mom. Acquired wealth is often your last chance to receive a large sum of money that, when invested wisely, can contribute to your becoming financially independent. Don't be foolish with your acquired wealth. You don't have to be nice to others who want to take advantage of you now that you have a few dollars in your pocket. More important, you don't have to feel guilty about getting the money. Spending it won't make you feel any better. And you definitely shouldn't blow it, because losing it will only make you feel worse!

COACHING TIPS

- **Spend a percentage of acquired wealth on whatever you want.** You can spend that portion on yourself, give it to a good cause, or share it with your children. Invest the remainder.
- **Put acquired wealth into a savings portfolio.** Don't keep it in your checking account, where you have easy access to it. Instead, invest it consistently with your investment strategy. If necessary, hire a financial professional to help you with developing a strategy. You'll find suggestions for how to find a reputable adviser in chapter 9.
- **Plan your charitable giving.** Anne Etheridge, executive director of the Norton Family Foundation in Santa Monica, California, is active in educating women about acquired wealth. Here's what she suggests when it comes to philanthropic giving:

  - Plan your philanthropic budget for the year. This gives you a guideline for how much to spend in any given month. Even if it's only ten dollars per month, it should be planned.
  - Consciously choose the causes to which you will contribute. You may be willing to give money to health-related issues but not to the arts. If you don't plan, you wind up giving away money to organizations you don't really want to fund.
  - Factor in "mad money." There's something to be said for spontaneity, so give yourself some room for things that may come up outside your regular budget.

Mistake 41

Being Risk-Averse

$\mathcal{A}$ study in the differences between the ways in which men and women invest money was conducted by Prudential Securities. They put investors into one of three zones: an action zone, a comfort zone, and a caution zone. It's no surprise that more men fell into the action zone and more women fell into the comfort and caution zones. Despite the fact that women are becoming increasingly empowered financially, study after study shows that they are more conservative and less inclined to take calculated risks than are men. The question of why this is true is evident in the facts that women have less money to invest in the first place and are less educated about investing.

Here are some examples of what we heard about women's investment-risk aversion:

I never fully learned that (a) to make money you have to spend money and (b) you can enjoy money. I've been working since I was thirteen and have always saved a sizable percentage of my income. I take comfort—maybe too much—in knowing I have a nest egg, but I'm not fully maximizing it.

I was afraid to invest in real estate. I always worried that as soon I invested, the market would collapse.

I've never taken enough risks with money. I've always carried around some mistaken notion that if I lost money I could never survive or that I would have to move out of the safety zone (where I belonged in the first place).

Every investment involves some level of risk. There are no guarantees. It's why you always see or hear that little disclaimer from investment firms that warns "These results may not predict or be typical of your results." On the other hand, no guts, no glory. The table below reveals that men are significantly more likely to take risks with the hope of turning that risk into profit. This isn't to say you should run out and make foolish or risky investments. It does mean that you've got to start sometime and there's no better time than now to find a trusted adviser with whom you can work.

WOMEN, MEN, and RISK

Willing to Take Substantial Risk for Substantial Gain	
Men	11%
Women	6%

Willing to Take Above-Average Risk for Above-Average Gain	
Men	30%
Women	19%

Source 2002 Equity Ownership in America, ICI/SIA

COACHING TIPS

- **Take baby steps.** If you're a new investor, don't take your entire nest egg out of the bank or from under the mattress and plunk it down in an investment. Get your feet wet by starting with some reasonable percentage of what's in the bank earning only 2 percent interest and putting it into a no-load or low-load mutual fund or other investment. Of course, you've got to do your research before even taking this move because no matter how small the amount, you want to minimize the risk.

- **Become educated.** I asked Katherine Wimmer, president of Wimmer Associates, a Pasadena, California, investment counseling firm, for some tips to help one become more comfortable with taking investment risks. She helps her own clients "demystify the process" by directing them toward educational resources. Katherine's suggestions are:

  - Join an investment club. Learn from other members, develop skills, gain confidence, socialize, and have fun.
  - Join the National Association of Investors Corporation. The cost is about $50 for an individual membership, and you can find them at www.better-investing.org.
  - Join the American Association of Individual Investors. Membership is $29 for basic service and includes a newsletter. Check them out at www.aaii.com.
  - Read the *Wall Street Journal*. Pay particular attention to the Getting Going column.
  - Use the New York Stock Exchange's free information available at www.nyse.com. Go to the site, then click on "About the NYSE," then click on "Education."

Mistake 42

Thinking You Don't Have Enough to Invest to Make a Difference

*F*rom Jakarta to Juneau, when women talk about the mistakes they make around money, they always include thinking that the amount they have to invest can't possibly put them on a path to wealth. Someone should have told that to Madame C. J. Walker, the first female millionaire in the United States! Walker, an African American, was born in Louisiana in 1867, soon after the abolition of slavery. She started off earning pennies a day as a washerwoman and, through pure determination and self-taught business savvy, parlayed that into a fortune she generously shared with others. In 1912, seven years before her death at the age of fifty-one, Walker told this to the National Negro Business League Convention:

> I am a woman who came from the cotton fields of the South. From there I was promoted to the washtub. From there I was promoted to the cook kitchen. And from there I promoted myself into the business of manufacturing hair goods and preparations . . . I have built my own factory on my own ground.

Thinking you don't have enough to make a difference is not only ridiculous, it's also dangerous. Such an attitude creates a catch-22. When you *believe* you don't have enough to invest, you *don't* invest, and remaining financially dependent becomes a certainty. Linda Stern, an investment writer for *Newsweek,* points out that a modest investment of $50 monthly (less than $13 a week or $2 a day) can yield $10,600 in ten years at historical stock market returns of 10.4 percent annually. Think about it. Fifty dollars a month is the amount you pay for morning coffee at Starbucks. One dinner at a good restaurant can cost you more than $50. For most women, coming up with $50 a month isn't a hardship and doesn't require deprivation. It does, however, require a shift in thinking from "If I don't have $1,000 or more to invest, it won't make a difference" to "Every little bit counts."

Regular investing allows you to optimize a concept called *dollar cost averaging*. Here's how it works. If you wait until you have $1,000 saved to buy a stock or mutual fund, you are paying for the value of that asset on the particular day you buy it. It could be high (in which case you're not getting as many shares for your money), or it could be low (in which case you're getting more for your money). But if you invest a smaller, fixed amount each month, you take advantage of the normal fluctuations in the market and, on average, will do better than with a larger lump sum investment.

If you're the kind of person who can't plant seeds in your garden because it takes too long to be gratified by their emergence, then investing small amounts will be hard for you. Investing small amounts monthly is like planting seeds rather than plants in bloom. It might seem as if it's just not making a big enough impact soon enough. But developing patience, not only in your financial life but in all aspects of your life, is the characteristic you need to cultivate if you want to live a more abundant life.

COACHING TIPS

- **Commit to an automatic $50 monthly withdrawal from your savings or checking account to a mutual fund.** You'll notice I specifically suggest it go into a mutual fund. Putting money from a checking account into a savings account isn't a bad idea, but given recent low returns in these accounts, it won't get you far. The automatic withdrawal is a surefire way to meet your commitment. Trust me, you won't even notice the money missing from your account.

- **Gradually increase the investment to $100 or more monthly.** Once you get in the investment habit and actually see your account grow, it will be easier to begin investing larger amounts. The positive reinforcement of watching your money yield even more money will become a fix you won't want to live without—I know because that's how I got hooked on the investment habit.

- **Plant some seeds.** I mean literally go out into your yard or buy a planter and plant seeds! There's no better way to learn patience than to nurture growth from seeds.

- **Check out low-fee, low-investment funds.** Stern suggests three funds that meet these criteria and that allow you to exit at any time: ABN Amro Mid Cap Fund, www.abnfunds.com; T. Rowe Price Capital Appreciation Fund, www.troweprice.com; and TIAA-CREF Equity Index Fund, www.tiaa-cref.org.

Mistake 43

Confusing Sentiment with Investment

*M*ore so than men, women have the tendency to attach sentiments to investments. These sentiments stem from various sources such as a memorable time when the investment was made, a person who recommended the investment, acquiring the investment through inheritance, or a personal relationship with a company represented in a portfolio. Women become emotionally attached to the investment as if it's the thread that keeps them connected with the person, time, or entity.

After the loss of a loved one, whether a mate, family member, or friend, some people inherit stocks, funds, or other investments contained in the deceased's portfolio. Many women come to look at these as "legacy" investments and are reluctant to tamper with them. At times it's because they believe the person willing it to them must have known what he or she was doing, and therefore leaving it as is would be the wisest thing to do. Other times it's sentiment that causes them to keep the investment.

It's not only sentiment involved with the passing of a loved one, but it can also be sentiment related to your own relationship with the stock or firm. Virginia is a case in point. In 1998, when she retired from GE after a long and successful career, she used a large portion of her retirement money to buy GE stock for her portfolio. She purchased the stock at $55 per share, and within a year it reached a ten-year high of nearly $60. Over the next several years she watched the stock decline to a low of just over $20, thereby losing more than half of her investment. Since this was money she was counting to live on in her "golden years," she has had to revise her plans and budget to accommodate the significantly reduced portfolio.

Maintaining investments for purely sentimental reasons can be a costly mistake—it's best not to keep all of your eggs in one basket. Before you run out and sell any of your assets, however, consult with a trusted investment adviser. This person can help you make decisions appropriate for your financial situation and identify any potential tax implications.

COACHING TIPS

• **Avoid "all or nothing" thinking.** If you see a sentimental investment begin to go down, don't feel as if you have to sell it all. After consulting with your investment team, consider selling off small portions at a time. This will allow you to remain connected to the investment but not lose such a large proportion of your equity.

• **Objectify acquired money.** Whether it's money you acquire through inheritance or retirement, distance yourself from the emotions surrounding it. Yes, it's a way to remain connected with a life or love lost, but it's also your future. You may not be able to do this immediately after the loss (and retirement is considered a loss too), but work toward approaching the inheritance in an objective, logical, and factual manner. Letting your financial future dwindle away isn't what your loved one would have wanted for you (or for his or her hard-earned money).

• **Keep an eye on your investment.** "Out of sight, out of mind" isn't the way to handle your investments. It may be difficult to regularly review your sentimental investments because they remind you of a loved one, but avoiding it will only make the future worse for you. If it's absolutely impossible for you to be objective about an inheritance, have a trusted financial adviser manage the money for you.

• **Diversify upon acquisition.** Rather than keep all your eggs in one basket, take large holdings in any one asset and divide them into smaller investments. One investment should not amount to more than 10 percent of your portfolio. Even though there may be tax ramifications, you may in the long run benefit from the diversification. A financial adviser can help you to make a good decision about what might be sold, what the tax basis would be, and if it's a wise move given your financial situation.

Mistake 44

Delaying the Purchase of a Home

*T*ypical homeowners generally have a higher net worth than renters," says Walter Molony, spokesperson for the National Association of Realtors. And to that I add, *if you're paying rent, you're never going to get rich.* Yes, I understand that women earn less and therefore it's harder to buy a home. Yes, I understand we dream of our first home as being the one into which our husbands will carry us over the threshold. And yes, with the soaring cost of real estate, I also realize that the thought of being solely responsible for repaying a debt of hundreds of thousands of dollars can be daunting. None of these excuses, however, are good enough to delay the benefit of home ownership.

I remember purchasing my own first home in 1979 as a single woman. It cost a whopping $74,000, and the interest rate was 16 percent. Add property tax impounds and the loan I had to repay that was part of the down payment, and I was paying more than $1,300 monthly. Was I scared? You betcha. But when I sold that house a year later for $100,000 and bought another one that I liked better for $119,000, delight replaced the fear. Ten years later I sold that one for just over $200,000. I continued doing this over the years to where I now own a home valued at well over a half million dollars—and all because I bought that first little starter home.

National census figures show that in 2001 nearly one-third of all home purchases were made by unmarried buyers. Even more impressive is that 18 percent of these buyers were single women and only 9 percent were single men. NBC money-matters expert Jean Chatzky urges women to look at home buying as a savings account. As you pay your mortgage bill month after month, you are also investing in your future. It's like forced savings. Historically, real estate maintains and grows in value. Reporting for the *Today* show, Chatzky tells women, "You may be scared, but you'll manage."

COACHING TIPS

• **Even if you're not ready to buy, shop anyway!** Cheryl Bouchard, ABR, Realtor with William Pitt Real Estate, a highly regarded Connecticut-based real estate company, suggests that you educate yourself about the housing market so that when you are ready to buy, you'll know desirable locations, what you're really looking for in a home, and other options related to becoming a homeowner. She also provides a few additional tips:

- Learn about financing options. There are actually ways to buy homes with little or nothing down.
- Keep your debt to income ratio low. Even if you have a good credit score, lenders will be looking at your existing debt.
- Consider getting a housemate. You can cut your mortgage in half and still be putting equity into your home.
- Don't wait for Prince Charming to buy the house with the white picket fence—buy it yourself.

• **Find out what you can afford.** Start with a visit to the Web site www.myfico.com. Here you can find out what your credit rating is, which in turn will help you determine how much money a bank would be willing to loan you and at what interest rate. Your credit rating is determined by a number of factors including how much money you currently owe, how many credit cards you have and use, and your repayment history. What many women don't know is that as their credit rating increases, the amount it costs to borrow money decreases. For example, a woman with a credit rating of 500 to 599 will pay over 9 percent interest on a loan amount of $150,000. A woman with a credit score of 720 to 850 will pay only 6 percent for that same loan. This is a difference of $332 monthly ($1,238 and $906, respectively).

- **Stretch yourself.** I learned that getting a loan outside of my comfort zone but within a range that I could afford paid dividends. Having to think twice before you buy that second pair of shoes isn't such a bad thing. Within a year or two you'll wonder why you ever worried in the first place.

- **Ask a friend for a referral to a Realtor.** Trusting and being comfortable with a Realtor is a critical part of the process. When I bought my last home, I interviewed a few people and settled on a team I really liked. I told them up front that I wasn't in a hurry because finding the right house was more important than finding one quickly. I even stipulated that I wanted them to e-mail me only the addresses of listings in my preferred geographic location and price range so that I could drive by them first, and if I wanted to go inside, I would call them to arrange to do so. I learned that there are computer systems that allowed them to do this automatically, whenever a home meeting my criteria was newly listed, so they weren't inconvenienced and I could look at it at my leisure.

- **Don't think your first home has to be your last.** This puts way too much pressure on the home buying process. Bouchard reminds women of the most important rule of real estate: location, location, location. Sometimes just getting into the market at a good time with a home you like but don't love is what you need to do. A fixer-upper could be a good deal for you, particularly if you can do the necessary remodeling or repairs yourself.

Mistake 45

Saving Instead of Investing

$\mathcal{O}$ne day over breakfast after an early morning television appearance, I asked my book publicist what she thought the biggest impediment to getting rich was for her. She thought for a moment, then replied, "I'm so afraid that I'm going to lose all my money that I just keep it all in an interest-bearing savings account." She isn't alone in this fear. A number of women we spoke with said the same thing. They were too cautious and didn't make their money grow. Sometimes they don't invest because they've been burned in the past. Others don't feel as if they have enough knowledge to be able to invest wisely. Whatever the reason, keeping your money in an interest-bearing account may be safe, but it's not wise.

"The key is understanding the difference between saving and investing," says Elizabeth Hoyle, vice president of marketing at Trimark Mutual Funds, in an interview with *Canadian Money Management Newsletter*. "Saving is accumulating your money, while investing is making that money work to earn more money. Savings earn a fixed amount of interest, but investments have the potential to grow."

There's another important aspect to investing, and that's diversification. You've heard the advice "Don't put all your eggs in one basket." You've probably also heard "Spread the wealth." Diversification is one of the greatest ways to do both and at the same time minimize your financial risk. All it means is that you should have a well-balanced portfolio of investments that are more likely to withstand trends and natural fluctuations in the financial market. Think of all the investors who shifted their money to the technology sector during the boom years of the 1990s. They made lots of money *on paper* but were caught frantically trying to develop a diversification strategy when that boom busted. One study suggests that by the time the average investor tries to adjust to changing market conditions, 80 percent of the damage is done.

COACHING TIPS

- **Get educated.** One of the main reasons why women don't invest as often as men is that they lack the knowledge necessary to feel comfortable doing so. The only way to overcome this fear is to become educated. Knowledge is power—particularly when it comes to money. One way to acquire knowledge is to join or start an investment club. The purpose of the club isn't to get rich quick, but rather to learn about investing with other women who share your interest in the topic. An article in the July 2004 issue of *Kiplinger's* magazine claims that there are only about half the number of investment clubs there were in 1997 and that the focus has shifted from making investments to education and socializing with like-minded women. This makes an investment club the perfect place to get up to speed on the meaning of investment jargon such as ROI, junk bonds, hedge funds, and debt ratio.

- **Find a female financial adviser.** Many women have difficulty talking to men about money because they are intimidated by what appears to be their wealth of knowledge (and often turns out to be just a line of B.S.). This isn't to say that women are better financial advisers, just that you might feel more comfortable having one educate you and handle your finances. To find a female financial adviser, start with getting a referral from a friend. If this fails, call several of the larger investment firms such as Schwab, Fidelity, American Express

Financial, or Merrill Lynch and ask to speak with a woman adviser. Before selecting one to work with, interview several, asking questions such as how long they have been in the field, how often they meet with their clients, what their approach to investing is, and what percentage of their clientele are women. You'll find more tips for finding an adviser, male or female, in chapter 9.

Mistake 46

Analysis Paralysis

*T*here's a certain kind of woman who makes this mistake. She tends to be perfectionistic, detail-oriented, logical, and analytical. She's not fearful of investing per se, she just wants to make sure she does it right. As a result, she collects information, talks to people, and analyzes what she should be doing—then doesn't do it. Having gathered so much information, she becomes overwhelmed and doesn't know what to do with it all. If you fall into this category, you must understand that there is no perfect investment strategy. If there were, everyone would follow it.

Waiting until you've found the ideal way to invest is a mistake because you delay accruing any return on your investment. We can't all be Warren Buffett. The goal is not to have the *perfect* strategy or even one that will yield the greatest results, but rather to have a *reasonable* one.

COACHING TIPS

• **Look into Target Maturity Funds.** For the person who can't decide what to do or who isn't really interested in managing a portfolio, Target Maturity Funds can provide an easy answer to the investment dilemma. American Century, Fidelity, T. Rowe Price, and Vanguard, among others, offer this option. Also called Lifecycle or Lifestyle Funds, this relatively new class of funds is designed to provide you with a diversified portfolio that is linked to your anticipated date of retirement. They are typically focused on more aggressive earnings during your younger years and automatically become more conservative as your retirement age approaches. Although they do not yield outstanding returns, they do provide reasonable ones.

• **Invest in U.S. savings bonds.** Again, the easy answer isn't always the most lucrative, but it's a start. There are a few different kinds of bonds available, and you want to carefully check the benefits of each before buying them, but all are guaranteed by the United States government and pay at least market rates. Some are even tax-free or allow for tax-deferred redemption. Savings bonds aren't sexy, but you can invest knowing you're not going to lose your shirt either.

Mistake 47

Relying on Social Security to Take You through Retirement

A recent Congressional Research Service report reveals that 61 percent of workers between twenty-four and sixty-four years old have *no retirement savings*. Unbelievably, nearly 54 percent of workers between fifty-five and sixty-four years old have no retirement savings, and the average amount in the accounts of those who do is only $57,331. If there's any good news in this at all, it's that the number of women saving for retirement is about the same as men. The bad news is that women live longer and take fewer investment risks—which means they will fall short of their retirement goals.

If you think the government is going to take care of you in your old age, think again. As baby boomers come to retirement age, the Social Security coffers will be challenged like never before in our country's history. Here are some eye-popping statistics I found on the Social Security Administration's Web site:

- 20 percent of older Americans rely on Social Security for 100 percent of their income.
- 33 percent of older Americans rely on Social Security for 90 percent or more of their income.
- 65 percent of older Americans rely on Social Security for 50 percent or more of their income.

Now couple that with these figures:

- In the year 2018 Social Security benefit payments will begin to exceed Social Security tax income.

- After the year 2042 the Social Security Trust Fund will be exhausted.

Those are startling and sobering statistics. If you're twenty-five years old today and planning to retire at age sixty-five, there's a good possibility there will be no money for you to draw on. Ask yourself if you are willing to put your financial future in the hands of Washington bureaucrats—no matter what their political affiliation. Use the chart below to see how you compare with other women with regard to how confident you are of having the amount of money you need to live comfortably in retirement.

WOMEN'S CONFIDENCE THAT THEY HAVE ENOUGH FOR RETIREMENT

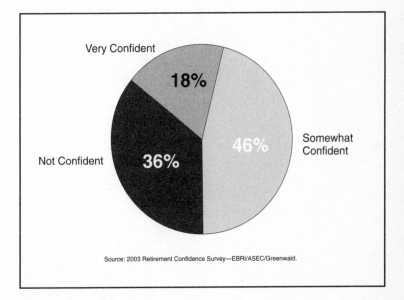

Source: 2003 Retirement Confidence Survey—EBRI/ASEC/Greenwald.

COACHING TIPS

• **Start saving *now*.** If you don't already have some kind of retirement or investment account *in your name* with *at least* your age **x** $2,000 in it, get going fast. It's never too early—or too late—to start accumulating your own wealth.

• **Increase funding to your retirement plan.** Some financial professionals suggest that you need twenty-five times your current annual income in savings to live comfortably in retirement. Most people aren't saving nearly enough today to meet this figure. Consider increasing your retirement plan contribution by at least 15 percent—and more if you can afford it.

Mistake 48

Not Taking Advantage of Compound Interest for Retirement

$\mathcal{B}$en Franklin described compounding as "the stone that will turn all your lead into gold." The keys to compounding are (1) regular savings, (2) reinvesting all dividends and earnings, (3) rate of return on your investment, and (4) leaving your investment untouched. Consider this:

- If at age twenty-five you put $100 per month into an account with an annual rate of return of 8 percent and didn't touch it until age fifty-five, you would have $146,815.04.
- If at age thirty you transferred your savings account of $10,000 into an investment account with an even more modest annual rate of return of 5 percent, then contributed just $200 per month until you reached age sixty, you would then have $394,256.65.
- If you're starting late and want to be a little more aggressive, let's say you begin at age forty by investing $500 per month in an investment account with an annual rate of return of 10 percent. At age sixty-five you would have $649,090.59.

As you can see, you don't have to be earning six figures to come up with what it takes to invest a reasonable amount in exchange for a healthy portfolio. This is not necessarily the same mistake as being risk-averse. There are plenty of women who are not risk-averse but still don't plan early in their lives to become financially free. Not investing soon enough was one of the most common themes heard from the women we talked to. Some were middle-aged who realized if they had only saved more, they wouldn't have to work at all, whereas others were older women who were working beyond the time they anticipated retiring because they hadn't saved soon enough.

COACHING TIPS

• **Consider retirement money sacrosanct.** Money that you save for retirement is different than a savings account. Savings accounts are for emergencies, travel, or major purchases. Your retirement account is just that—money to be used only in retirement. Withdrawal is often less tempting if you keep this money in an IRA or other form of retirement fund that will penalize you for withdrawal before a certain age. You want compound interest to be working for you from an early age.

• **Invest early.** You cannot start investing for retirement early enough, and it's unlikely that you will contribute often enough. From the time you get your very first paycheck you should be making contributions to a retirement account that over your working life will compound exponentially.

• **Invest often.** Don't restrict yourself to making investments monthly, quarterly, or annually. Similarly, don't wait until you feel you have a large enough sum of money to deposit into your account. Remember, compounding works with every single dollar you invest from the moment it goes into your account. You can capitalize on compound interest by investing at every opportunity.

Mistake 49

Not Leveraging Company Contributions

*E*ven if you have your own individual retirement account (IRA), a company pension plan, or other retirement savings, you're just plain foolish if you don't take advantage of a company-sponsored 401(k) plan. Many companies offer both pension plans and 401(k) plans, so don't think you are entitled to only one or the other or that you need to participate in only one plan. The difference between the two is that a traditional pension plan pays a fixed amount after retirement (usually based on years of service and salary) and the company controls how the money is invested, whereas the 401(k) plan allows employees to contribute a portion of their paycheck with pretax dollars to a retirement fund.

The 401(k) also allows the employee to select how the money is to be invested among the choices offered by the company, such as mutual funds, money market accounts, and the company's stock. Probably the greatest advantage of many 401(k) plans is that the employer matches all or part of your contribution. You don't have to do anything other than enroll in the plan to receive the company's contribution, and you pay no taxes on their contribution (or yours) until you retire, so this can be considered "free money" that will grow tax-deferred. Employers vary on how much they contribute, so check to see what your company offers.

When I first started working for a corporation, they had such a plan available, but at twenty-six years old I thought retirement was too far off for me to sign up for it. Duh! I missed out on nearly three years of free money—money the company would have put into my account at no cost to me.

When I finally left the company seven years after enrolling in the company 401(k) plan, I was able to transfer more than $30,000 into a private retirement plan. This was in addition to the pension I earned that will be available to me when I turn fifty-nine years old. Not bad for seven years of painless investing.

Company-sponsored 401(k) plans are the ideal way to start saving for retirement. Benefits include:

- Even though you get to choose where your money goes, your company has someone managing your investment.
- There are frequently matching contributions from your company.
- It's automatic—comes right out of your paycheck before you even get the chance to spend it in your mind.
- It's protected by ERISA laws.
- By allowing you to invest pretax dollars, your taxable income is lowered.

COACHING TIPS

- **Starting today, contribute the *maximum allowed* into your company 401(k) plan.** In 2005 the maximum you are allowed to contribute to a 401(k) plan is $14,000 annually. That increases to $15,000 in 2006 and, as of this writing, increases in $500 increments each year thereafter. Remember, that's pretax earnings, which means your taxable income is reduced by the amount you contribute, so not only do you invest the $14,000 but you also reduce the amount you pay in income taxes.
- **Use your raises to increase your contribution.** If contributing the maximum puts too much of a strain on your

budget, put the money you receive from an annual merit raise or promotion directly into your 401(k) plan. You'll always spend the amount you get in your paycheck, so don't tempt yourself with that raise. This is a smart way to remain at your current standard of living yet up the ante on your retirement funds.

• **Consult a financial adviser about the best way to invest your 401(k) money.** As mentioned earlier, the right financial professional can help you maximize earnings by suggesting diversified investments and investments with a degree of risk appropriate for your age (your risk should decrease with age).

Mistake 50

Paying Off "Good Loans" Early

 $\mathcal{N}$ ot all debt is created equal. Credit card debt does you no good. But car loans, home loans, and business loans, depending on your situation, might not be such a bad thing. Many women will accelerate payments on loans that have tax-saving benefits, but they continue to carry charges on their credit cards. They typically do so because they're uncomfortable having a larger amount hanging over their heads while the smaller amounts aren't as troublesome to them.

Angela was one such woman. She had about $5,000 in credit card debt and an outstanding mortgage on her home of $57,000. She got it into her head that she wanted to own her home free and clear and paid as much as she possibly could each month on her mortgage, but only the minimum on her charge cards. There are three reasons why this would be considered a mistake:

1. The interest on her home loan was tax-deductible, and in her tax bracket she could use all the deductions she could get to offset her high salary. Paying off her home loan would result in paying higher income taxes.
2. The extra money she was putting into her home loan could have been invested, thereby yielding more money in her pocket in the long run.
3. By paying just the minimum on her charge cards, she was actually accruing more debt in the form of interest that could not be used as a tax deduction.

It's tempting, and even admirable, to want to live free of debt, but there are times when the interest paid on loans can work to your benefit. Think twice about paying off loans just for the convenience of it—in the end it can wind up costing you more.

COACHING TIPS

- **Get tax advice.** If you're not sure whether it's more advantageous to keep an outstanding balance on a loan, ask a tax professional. The amount you pay for a consultation could be a great investment.
- **Get a home equity line of credit.** Many women aren't aware that the interest paid on a home equity line of credit can be tax-deductible. If you own a home and have credit card debt, you're better off using a line of credit to pay off the debt. Not only is the interest rate often lower, you might also be able to write it off.
- **Always pay off credit card debt first.** Most interest paid on credit cards is not only exorbitantly high, it's also not tax-deductible. This makes it critical that you avoid carrying *any* credit card debt or at least that you pay it off as soon as possible.

Mistake 51

Not Seeking Financial Advice

$\mathcal{R}$esearch shows that women are more reluctant to spend money on consultants and advisers than are men. Reasons for this include not having the money to spend, not knowing whom to trust, not wanting to spend the money on themselves, and not knowing the questions to ask of an adviser. They're all legitimate concerns, but it's important to understand that financial advisers take many shapes and forms. There are certainly professional advisers who make a living from helping you to accumulate wealth, but there are also plenty of other people in your life who can provide you with advice or guidance as well. Whom you choose to give you advice is not as important as getting advice when you need it, provided they are trustworthy, objective, and have your best interests at heart. In this regard, I think of it as more of a financial coach—someone who can help you to achieve peak financial performance.

I recall when my father died and my mother was left to manage the modest portfolio he left to her. She began asking me questions at a time in my life when I really paid no attention to my own finances. I was so busy *earning* money that I wasn't taking the time to manage it and make it grow. I suggested that she hire a financial adviser to help her, but being an independent sort of woman, and one who was reluctant to spend money on the unknown, she chose to go another route. She found financially secure people around her and used them as her advisers. But she didn't just rely on their advice. Instead, she began reading books, newspapers, and articles related to investment planning so that she could ask informed questions and judge the reliability of the advice she received.

As a result, she successfully grew that modest portfolio to where she didn't have to worry about money for the remainder of her life.

In her book *Secrets of Six-Figure Women: Surprising Strategies to Up Your Earnings and Change Your Life* (HarperBusiness, 2004), Barbara Stanny writes, "Success is not a solitary journey. Ask any six-figure woman. They constantly spoke of the significance of other people to their financial success." Stanny took the information gleaned from the research she conducted with six-figure women and created two distinct categories of advisers: "true believers" and "way showers." Whereas the former are people who believe in you and your capabilities and are there to cheer you on to success, the latter are people with the technical know-how to show you how to get there.

Whether you choose to hire someone or seek guidance from trusted family or friends, the important thing is to use others as resources for becoming better informed, making solid decisions, and beginning the process of taking charge of your wealth—no matter how large or small it may be currently. Admit what you don't know and be open to wise counsel.

COACHING TIPS

• **Identify the kind of advisers you need for your stage of financial planning.** If you're at the beginning of your path to wealth, you probably don't need to pay someone to help you. You can start by speaking to friends or family, reading, going to seminars, or connecting with a reputable investment firm that will be paid through commissions from your investments. On the other hand, if you've acquired or inherited a significant amount of wealth, you should consider an investment adviser—preferably one who is paid a percentage of your portfolio and not from commissions.

- **Create your financial coaching team.** Think about the people around you who can be of help. One person can't be all things to you, so identify several people who can fill the roles of educating you, helping you analyze your investments, assisting you with selecting an investment firm, and answering basic questions about creating wealth. Ask each person if she would be willing to spend an hour a month with you to share her experiences, the mistakes she's made along the way, and some of her wisest decisions.

- **Interview several advisers before selecting one.** In Mistake 14 and chapter 9 you will find more detailed discussions of what to look for in a financial adviser, but here are a few questions you should consider asking him or her:

  - What are your areas of specialization?
  - How long have you been offering financial planning and/or investment counseling services to clients?
  - What is your education and what certification designations do you possess?
  - Will you provide me with references from other professionals?
  - How many clients do you work with?
  - Would I work with you or with an associate of yours?
  - How is your firm compensated, and how is your compensation determined?
  - Do you have an agreement describing your compensation and services that will be provided in advance of the engagement?
  - If you earn commissions, approximately what percentage of your firm's income comes from this?

- Are there any financial incentives for you to recommend certain investments or products to clients?

- **Maintain control of your portfolio.** Whether you hire an investment adviser or use an investment firm, avoid the inclination to turn it all over to them and wash your hands of responsibility. No matter how professional and trustworthy these people may be, they have many portfolios to oversee and you can't expect them to pay as close attention to your money as you can yourself. Meet regularly with your professional adviser to review your portfolio and make necessary changes.

Mistake 52

Not Planning for Unexpected Disability

$\mathcal{B}$ecoming disabled isn't something we want to think about at any age, but failing to do so can rob you of your entire life savings. Kathryn Black, an estate planning attorney in California, shared with me how this happened to one woman with whom she worked. Abby was thirty-seven when she was seriously injured in a car accident. While she was hospitalized and in a coma for twelve weeks her bills piled up, but there was no one who was authorized to handle her financial affairs. Her family filed in court to have a guardian appointed to act on her behalf, but Abby's siblings couldn't agree on just who should be appointed. In the meantime, the court proceedings became lengthy and costly. After a period of time, she recovered and was able to resume handling her own finances but had to terminate the guardianship through the courts. Not only did she lose wages and have huge medical bills, but she also had to pay attorney fees and costs relating to the guardianship and its termination.

Conversely, Kathryn worked with another woman, Harriet, a forty-two-year-old divorcée with no children. Having the foresight to know that she needed someone she could trust to handle her finances if she were to become incapacitated, she gave her brother authority to act as her agent under a power of attorney. His authority to act would begin only if Harriet became unable to act for herself and would terminate if she regained her capacity. No expensive court proceedings were required, and for a nominal fee she had the peace of mind that comes from knowing one's financial house is in order.

COACHING TIPS

- **Consider purchasing disability insurance.** If you can afford to be off from work for an indefinite amount of time and continue with the lifestyle you currently have, support your family, and maintain your home, then you don't need disability insurance. On the other hand, if you're like most people, a serious illness or disability can mean financial disaster, including the loss of your home and savings. If your employer offers it as part of your compensation package, buy it. If you're self-employed, look into the different types available and how much they cost, then make an informed decision about what would best protect you and your assets.

- **Set aside money to cover your expenses until benefits kick in.** Every woman should have in an emergency account at least the amount of money to pay for six months of household expenses in the event of catastrophe—disability or otherwise.

- **Appoint a trusted friend or family member to act under a power of attorney in the event of incapacitation.** This is a relatively simple procedure to complete. You can even go online to www.legalzoom.com and get all the forms needed to do it yourself. The most important factor here is to select someone you trust and upon whom you can rely to act on your behalf in the manner you instruct. If you're not comfortable completing the forms yourself, it's worth paying for one visit to an attorney.

Chapter Seven

Maximizing Your Financial Potential at Work

Power is the strength and the ability to see yourself through your own eyes and not through the eyes of another. It is being able to place a circle of power at your own feet and not take power from someone else's circle.

LYNN V. ANDREWS

For those of us who work for a living, and I would wager to say that's most people reading this book, the workplace can be a huge source of not only financial wealth but perks, benefits, and other things that can contribute to a wealthy lifestyle. If you've already read *Nice Girls Don't Get the Corner Office: 101 Unconscious Mistakes Women Make That Sabotage Their Careers*, you know that in that book I provide hundreds of tips for how you can achieve your career goals, which in turn help you to increase your quality and standard of living. The book covers everything from how to ask for a raise if you think you've been overlooked to ways to approach your work so that you have time to engage in the activities you most enjoy—both of which are important aspects of leading a rich life.

When considering your pay, benefits, perks, or the corner office, ask yourself whether you have what you want, what you deserve, and what others have. If the word *greedy* comes to mind, exorcise it from your vocabulary. Women who worry that they're just being greedy are usually the last ones who *should* be worrying about it. Greedy people don't think of themselves as greedy. They simply insist on receiving everything they think is due them—which is usually more than they deserve in actuality, and that's why we call them greedy! The tips in this chapter don't suggest that you ask for more than you deserve, but they do challenge you to move away from the notion that it's better to wait to be given what you've earned than to ask for it, and to move toward behaviors that will bring you closer to a rich life.

Keep in mind that living a rich life isn't only about acquiring money, although that's a large part of it. It's also about living the lifestyle that you want. All too often women allow themselves to be taken advantage of in the workplace. They don't ask for the things they deserve, gravitate toward lower-paying professions, and too willingly make concessions that detract from their lifestyles. That's why this chapter includes ways you can earn more money, save more money, have more free time, or in other ways enhance your lifestyle yet pay little or nothing for those enhancements.

Mistake 53

Working in a Female Ghetto

$\mathcal{T}$he good news is, you got a degree. The bad news is, you can't make any money with it. I use the term *female ghettos* to describe the many fields where workers remain underpaid and undervalued because they are populated primarily with women. Nursing, elementary education, social work, and administration are all examples of fields that are historically low-paying precisely because of the presence of large numbers of women. The more women in a field, the more likely the pay scale will be artificially lowered.

What these fields also have in common is that they are "helping" professions. The primary duty of the women (and men) who perform these roles is to be of assistance to others, as opposed to providing a professional service, making a product, or contributing technical know-how. And who in our society are socialized to be helpers? Of course—women. Dr. Lois Joy, an economist and researcher with the Women's Faculty Forum at Yale University, has conducted research into the fields women and men choose as professions. There is little difference, she found, between the majors women and men choose in college. Women today are much more likely than twenty years ago to major in business, the sciences, mathematics, and engineering. Despite this fact, women and men are concentrated in different professions. In 1995 women comprised 93 percent of all nurses, 84 percent of all elementary school teachers, and less than 1 percent of all engineers. In the same year women still outnumbered men in the clerical and service occupations, while men outnumbered women in labor and production occupations. This occupational segregation accounts for a large share of the male-female wage gap.

And what does all this mean for you? If you want to get rich, you're going to have a quicker time of it if you prepare yourself for fields that are not gender-segregated. So if you're currently working toward a degree, think about whether it's really going to give you the ultimate income and lifestyle you want. If you've already been through college and have that degree in childhood education in hand, not to worry. It's never too late (or too early) to choose a field that will bring you both satisfaction and the quality of life to which you aspire. Career changers are no longer viewed as fickle or lacking direction. It's expected that twenty-something workers will have multiple careers over their work lives.

All of this isn't to say you can't get rich being a teacher, social worker, or nurse, because you can. You're just going to have a steeper hill to climb because you're not going to make as much money as you would in business, sales, manufacturing, or law. Not interested in those fields? Already integrated into one of these "helping" professions? Let me give you some ideas for how you can combine what does interest you with a higher-paying job.

COACHING TIPS

• **Lose the notion that doing good and doing well are mutually exclusive.** Too many women believe that the only way they can make a contribution to society is to live like Mother Teresa. There's no crime in making money while you serve others. If you're already in a "helping" field but aren't satisfied with the richness of your life, give yourself permission to explore alternatives. Since sometimes this can be the hardest thing to do, you might want to consult with a career counselor to see the array of options before you.

• **Don't let your college degree determine your future.** Just because you majored in the classics doesn't mean you can't become the next Ted Turner. In fact, Ted Turner *did* major in the classics. And Carly Fiorina, CEO of Hewlett-Packard, majored in medieval history and philosophy, actress Lisa Kudrow in biology, and Janet Reno in chemistry. After your first few jobs, hiring managers will focus more on what you achieved in your last position than on what you studied.

• **Use your *money* to do good.** When I first became so busy in my profession that I didn't have time to give to the causes in which I believe, I felt guilty. I felt guilty because I was busy making money and not taking the time to make a difference in the lives of those who couldn't afford my fees or services. Now, this is definitely classic "girl" guilt. But instead of donating my time, I started donating copies of my books, money to fund scholarships for inner-city schoolgirls and feeding the hungry, and contributing to start-ups that serve women and girls (the causes that are most important to me). When I can, I also provide pro bono training programs or keynote addresses. Wealthy women are in a unique position to give significant amounts of financial resources to good causes—something that is every bit as valuable as giving your time to them.

The following coaching tips are from Judy Estrin, president of Partners in Enterprise, Inc., a Burbank, California, consulting, performance improvement, and training firm that works with individuals, start-up entrepreneurs, and corporations in achieving their strategic goals through pragmatic and innovative leadership:

• **Find a specialty within your field that is going to be needed by other professionals.** Be the only one in your organization who can provide that specialty. For example, if you're an administrative professional, become the expert on making high-quality PowerPoint presentations. Or if you work in the accounting department, research the best practices of others in your field and devise a system that incorporates these. Then develop a training program and become a consultant to others in your specialty area. You may be able to "go on the road" with a training program a couple of days a month, keep your day job, and make as much from your consulting as you do from your day-to-day work.

• **Look to your volunteer life to be where your helping side is fulfilled.** If your current job allows you to make a good living, but not make a difference, you don't have to quit it. Make a difference by volunteering with those organizations that complement your values.

• **Don't be afraid to go into management.** Being the boss can also mean being in the bonus pool in addition to having a larger base salary.

• **Not-for-profit does not mean not-for-pay.** Learn good business management skills and apply them. When Elizabeth Dole was head of the Red Cross, she was compensated at a respectable $200,000 annually (which she chose not to collect her first year at the helm), and her successor was paid twice that amount.

• **Following your heart path does not mean you need to be poor.** If you have a message, consider writing books or making documentaries or producing shows/films that have meaning— and turn a profit at the bookstore or the box office.

Mistake 54

Working at a Salary Less Than What You Deserve

𝒟eborah Kolb and Judith Williams, authors of *The Shadow Negotiation* (Simon & Schuster, 2000), estimate that women lose in excess of $520,000 during the course of their careers. Among the ways this happens is our inclination to trade pay for flexible working schedules and, as mentioned earlier, to gravitate toward nonprofit organizations rather than higher-paying corporations. In my own work with women I see it all the time. Women are given additional assignments and moved to new jobs with the promise of more money, but that money often never materializes. What's worse, they won't confront the problem or negotiate a raise. We need to be better at using the now famous line uttered over and over by Cuba Gooding in the movie *Jerry Maguire:* "Show me the money!"

Most of us have heard the statistic that women earn only seventy-seven cents for each dollar earned by men. What we don't usually hear is that this disparity is even bigger when it comes to compensation for non-Caucasian women. The following chart shows you that the salaries of African American women and Latinas are far lower than even those of their Caucasian female counterparts. If you fall into either of these groups, you owe it to yourself to know the value of your position in the open market and to negotiate for that amount with your current employer or find an employer who will pay you what you're worth.

Salary Comparison by Ethnicity

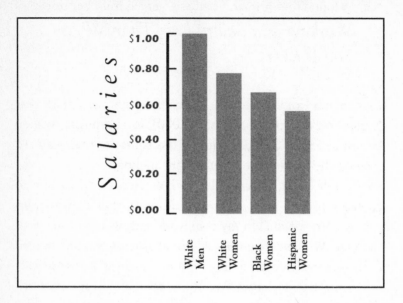

I had the pleasure of interviewing Dr. Lisa Barron, an assistant professor in organizational behavior at the Graduate School of Management at the University of California, Irvine. Lisa published an article, "Ask and You Shall Receive: Gender Differences in Negotiators' Beliefs about Requests for a Higher Salary," based on a study she conducted with male and female MBA students from a major university in the United States.

The scenario involved all students being offered a job with a salary of $61,000 and a bonus of $5,000. They were also told that other students from their program were offered similar jobs at another company with a salary of $67,000 and a bonus of $10,000. The students in the study were given information that would allow them to negotiate not only their salaries but also tuition reimbursement and vacation. In the end both men and women negotiated for more money, but men wound up receiving significantly more—because they *asked* for more. Barron found four primary themes emerged from her research:

1. Entitlement: The men felt they were entitled to even more than what their colleagues had been offered at the other company, whereas the women felt it would be "fair" to get equal to what their colleagues received. In other words, men had more of a sense of entitlement and women more of a desire to ask for what they thought was fair.

2. Worth: The men equated their salaries more with what they thought they were worth. If a colleague was receiving $67,000 annually, they believed they should get more because they were worth more. Women were uncomfortable with the notion of worth, didn't think of themselves as worth more, or couldn't measure their worth.

3. Proving oneself: The women in the study were hesitant to ask for more money before they could prove they deserved it, whereas the men used past experience as a rationale for getting more money.

4. Consequences: Both men and women considered the consequences of asking for more money, but men were concerned that possibly damaging the relationship in the present could hurt them down the road. But the women were more worried that the recruiter would think poorly of them or think they were greedy or not nice.

What does all this mean? One of the most obvious and measurable ways in which women sabotage their efforts to get rich is their unwillingness to ask for what they want, deserve, or need. Barron offers great coaching tips for what to do about it, so read on.

COACHING TIPS

Barron provides these suggestions for how you can better negotiate for pay, but they apply equally to negotiations related to just about anything:

- **Gather data.** When it comes to salary negotiations, get lots of information about the job market, your position, and salary range. You can get this data from your alumni center, online, networks you belong to, or professional associations. Consider calling someone in another company with similar positions and say something like, "Do you think [specify amount] is a good salary for this position?" Be careful not to speak only with women—they're already getting paid less than men! The Web site www.salary.com can provide you with information about the salary range for practically any job you can name and sorts the information by geographic location. The basic service is free, but for a fee they will provide you with a more detailed report based on your specific skills.

- **Work on your sense of entitlement.** Keep a *weekly* list of accomplishments (not monthly or yearly). Pay particular attention to anything that has to do with money: How much did you earn? Save? Spend? Talk with someone you trust who can give you an accurate picture of yourself and your achievements. Women tend to be more self-deprecating about accomplishments, which doesn't help to enhance their sense of entitlement. If you're going into salary negotiations and you don't think you're entitled, you will reveal this in your speech and body language. You've got to walk in *believing* you deserve what you're asking for.

- **Assess your skill set.** Are you above average? Have you done things that people in your field haven't done? Do you have unique qualities, skills, education, or experiences? Have you managed a huge budget? Do you speak Japanese? If you have above-average or hard-to-find skills, then you *should* be asking for more than what others are paid on the average.

• **Be objective.** The kind of argument you make for more money has to be objective. Turn "I work hard" into "Last year I managed a team of fifty people and implemented an entire new set of policies and procedures that helped turn the company from not profitable to profitable." Rather than saying, "I'm committed and have proved myself," focus on facts. Make your case by articulating what you did better, faster, cheaper, with fewer errors or less hassle than the next person. Being comfortable when talking about your objective achievements brings success . . . and it's *not* bragging. If you don't toot your own horn, no one will know you're in the band!

Mistake 55

Neglecting the Perks

$\mathcal{P}$erks are benefits that people get *in addition to* company-sponsored plans like health insurance, disability, vacation, and retirement plans. Benefits are typically provided under the provisions of formal company policy—which you may or may not be able to influence. For example, you may earn three weeks of vacation with your current employer because you've worked the number of years that entitle you to it, but you're making a move to a new employer where you start out earning only two weeks for the first few years. Whereas larger corporations often have inflexible rules that apply to all employees, smaller employers may be willing to negotiate for the right person. Overlooking benefits and perks when negotiating for a new job can deprive you of benefits to which you may be entitled, or ones you could negotiate into your total compensation package, if you only ask. These can add as much as 40 percent to your base salary.

Some perks to consider are:

- A company car
- Training programs
- Sign-on bonus
- Stock options
- Accelerated review and accompanying raise
- Child care
- Club membership

A caveat here is to not even consider negotiating for perks until after you've received a salary offer. It could be that the salary offer is so good you won't need to negotiate for many perks. On the other hand, if it's so low that you might not even consider the job, the perks may just make the offer more appealing—particularly if it's from an employer you particularly want to work for or if the job is one you really want.

COACHING TIPS

• **Accentuate the positive.** Let the person you're negotiating with know that you appreciate his or her offer and that you are hoping to add a few things to the overall compensation package.

• **In addition to the perks that are important to you, ask for some you can live without.** You don't want to come in with a long laundry list of negotiable items, but you do want to have an item or two that you can "give in on" to make it a win-win situation with the employer.

• **Summarize your understanding of the offer in writing.** After an agreement has been reached, send your new employer a letter expressing your enthusiasm about beginning work with them and restating the financial arrangements. Without making it sound like a legal document, simply say you want to confirm your understanding of the offer.

• **Be willing to walk away.** Negotiating for salary and benefits can be like negotiating for the car of your dreams. Once you get caught up in the emotions, you might not cut the best deal for yourself. Rather than agree to any offer on the spot, ask for time to think about it. Speak with friends, do some follow-up research if necessary, then make a decision. In the long run you'll never be happy working for an employer who you think gave you short shrift financially.

• **Read *The Wetfeet Insider Guide to Negotiating Your Salary and Perks.*** It's filled with great tips for knowing how and what to negotiate with an employer. You can purchase it online at www.wetfeet.com.

Mistake 56

Not Getting Reimbursed for Out-of-Pocket Expenses

This mistake ties in closely with "Pinching Company Pennies," a mistake I wrote about in *Nice Girls Don't Get the Corner Office*. In an effort not to "nickel-and-dime" your employer to death, you may be reluctant to submit an expense report for the five dollars you spent on office supplies, the eight-dollar cab ride, or the twelve dollars you spent on bagels for the staff meeting. Each of those expenses alone won't make you rich (or poor), but when you add them up over the course of a year, you'll find they can amount to a significant amount of money. "For each receipt you misplace, that's money you've thrown away," says Christine DiTullio Reiter, president of Time Finders. "I have found that people who postpone their expense reports for weeks and months at a time really lose money. The greater amount of time that passes between the return from a trip and completion of an expense report, the greater amount of money lost. This trait [of postponing/procrastinating] is very common among people who have cluttered offices and desks."

Besides just being disorganized, many women don't expense these work-related costs because they are more likely than men to be concerned about making a negative impression when they spend company money—even on legitimate expenditures. Men, on the other hand, know that these expenses are simply "the cost of doing business" and don't hesitate to use their departmental budget.

And there's yet another reason why women don't submit those expenses. It's because they're so busy doing things like making miracles, helping colleagues with *their* work, and working well beyond the company baseline for hard work (mistakes that are also explained in *Nice Girls Don't Get the Corner Office*) that they don't have the time to keep track of them! Self-employed women are equally guilty of failing to track their expenses. Combine these two reasons with the fact that women are sometimes hesitant to have their administrative staff prepare their expense reports, and it results in women shortchanging themselves one more time.

Getting reimbursed does require a certain amount of record keeping and completion of paperwork, but if you make time to go the extra mile for your employer, then you should also be taking equally good care of yourself. The coaching tips below will help you to simplify the record keeping and reimbursement process.

COACHING TIPS

• **Keep all work-related receipts in one place.** It can be as simple as a file in your desk labeled "Receipts." Once a week (or more often) go through your purse or wallet and put all receipts for work expenses in the file. Keeping them in one place increases the likelihood that you'll make time to file that expense report.

• **Create an Excel spreadsheet to help you keep a tally of your expenses.** Using the categories your company suggests for tracking expenses (e.g., meals and entertainment, office supplies, ground transportation), create a spreadsheet where you can enter your expenditures. You have to do this only once, so it's worth the time you put into it. Then, on a monthly basis (or more frequently if your company requires it for payment), block out time on your calendar to transfer the amounts in your receipts file to the spreadsheet.

- **Submit your expense reports regularly, but only as often as the company requires you to do so.** Once you start submitting them regularly, you'll notice just how much money you've been giving away to your employer (or if you're self-employed, to the government)! It's a waste of your time, though, to submit expense reports more often than necessary to ensure reimbursement, and it doesn't give you the opportunity to "bundle" expenses together.

DiTullio Reiter offers these specific tips for those who travel on business and encounter many nonreceipted expenses:

- **Keep envelopes labeled by trip name in your handbag (versus briefcase).** This way, receipts can be dropped in the envelope at the same time the credit card or wallet, if it is a cash transaction, is put back in the purse.
- **While the pen is in hand for signing a charge slip, jot a quick note of any pertinent information on the receipt.** For example, when you pay parking fees, you're given a receipt (and if you're not, ask for one). That receipt does not reflect the tip you gave the valet when the car was delivered, so make a note of it on the receipt. Or, when checking out of a hotel, write down on the receipt the amount you left for the maid, paid the concierge for a special service, or tipped the bellman for getting you a cab.
- **Take advantage of technical tools for tracking.** PalmOne PDAs have Excel-compatible software on board. Expenses can be entered in the proper columns as they are incurred. This is even better because many corporations have expense reports set up in an Excel format. That means that when you return from the trip, syncing the Palm with the company expense form is a piece of cake—and a done deal (or expense report) as soon as one returns!

Mistake 57

Giving Away Your Time

$\mathcal{T}$he opposite of working in a female ghetto is working in a field where you should be making a good living but you're not. When I recently went for a doctor's appointment, my female physician asked what I was working on and I told her about *Nice Girls Don't Get Rich*. She shook her head and said, "That's especially true for women doctors. It's well known that we earn less than men doing the same work." Her remark surprised me, so I did a little research into pay disparity among people in traditionally high-paying fields.

Census Bureau reports and surveys of young physicians indicate that male physicians indeed earn more than female physicians, even after differences in the number of hours worked, specialty, practice setting, and other characteristics are taken into account. Similarly, male lawyers earn a median income of $90,000, according to recent Census Bureau statistics, whereas women lawyers earn $66,000. Thinking about it further, I realized it makes sense that there would be these wage gaps. A woman is just as likely to act like a "girl" whether she's a doctor, lawyer, psychologist, or CPA as is a woman in any other field.

There are a couple of ways this happens. In the case of physicians women tend to spend more time with their patients, focusing on their emotional, not just physical, needs. This results in seeing fewer patients in a day, hence less income. Similarly, because they are focused on patient care, they often neglect the business details (such as coding or billing) that would boost their incomes. And physician moms face all the same problems encountered by their corporate counterparts—they have to take time off to care for sick kids, pick up kids from school, and so on. Women attorneys are in the same position. Eager to provide their clients with "value," they shortchange themselves when it comes to balancing the needs of others and their own financial well-being. As a result, these female professionals wind up working longer hours and making less money.

Giving away time, hence money, doesn't happen only in professions such as law and medicine. It happens to women at every range of the economic spectrum. From the salaried accounting manager who receives no overtime pay but is forced to stay late because she's asked to help out a less experienced colleague, to the day-care provider who waits well beyond the time children should be picked up because a parent is stuck in a meeting, women leave thousands of dollars on the table because they so willingly give away their time. If you can relate to this problem, I encourage you to take advantage of the following coaching tips.

COACHING TIPS

• **Create time boundaries.** There's a saying: Work expands to fill the time available. Be clear about the amount of time you can spend with your patients, clients, colleagues, or customers and still be able to make money. Providing superior service does not mean giving away your time and resources. It's not the *amount* of time spent that matters, it's the *quality* of the time you give that makes the difference. If your appointment is for thirty minutes, then stick with it. Not only does it keep you on schedule so that you can see the maximum number of people possible in a day, it lets all those people you serve know that you're equally concerned about *their* time and not keeping them waiting.

• **Learn your business.** Every business has its own ins and outs and tricks of the trade. You don't have to reinvent the wheel, but you do need to know how to run the business side of your profession in a way that maximizes profits. It may mean taking a class or hiring a consultant to help you. My own physician mentioned that one of the reasons she doesn't make the same amount of money as the male colleagues she shares an office with is that they have taken the time to memorize all the billing codes. So they are able to submit an invoice for payment more quickly, and it's less likely to be rejected for having a wrong code. She sheepishly admits that she isn't as familiar with the codes as her colleagues because she chooses to spend the time it would take to learn the codes with patients and her children and family.

• **Keep track of billable hours.** When I started my own consulting firm, I was like many women who are so busy wanting to help people that they often neglect to keep track of the number of billable hours amassed during a day or week. I'm sure I cheated myself out of tens of thousands of dollars as a result. No more! I keep track of the time spent on every billable call or meeting and send it to the woman in our office who does the billing so that I can be paid for my services—just as I pay for the services of others.

Mistake 58

Reducing Your Fees or Prices

*T*his mistake is another one I'm guilty of. One of the reasons I didn't acquire the wealth I wanted earlier was that I let my emotions rule my fee schedule. The people in my office have taught me to laugh over the fact that there are clients I've worked with for fifteen years for whom I feel compelled to honor the original fee that was quoted to them—fifteen years ago! Similarly, a therapist friend of mine often talks about ways in which her soft spot for clients has prevented her from getting rich. In some instances, when she has lowered the hourly fee so that a client can afford to see her, she later finds out the client just bought a new BMW or second home in the Hamptons. Or she'll agree to wait for payment until the client receives his insurance reimbursement, only to have him keep it when his therapy ends.

Placing too high a value on relationships or thinking with your heart and not your business acumen can cause you to lose out on what is legitimately yours. If you own a shop and give your friends products at cost, you are actually losing money. The price of the item is only part of what goes into the sales price. Your overhead, time spent buying, and money spent on building a relationship with a vendor are but a few of the other parts to consider in pricing. In the same way, if you provide a service at an hourly fee, it's not your time the person is paying for. It's the years of education and experience that went into accumulating the knowledge or skill to be an expert in that service. You made an investment in yourself, and cutting your fee reduces the return on that investment. I've learned the hard way—a woman typically doesn't get rich by cutting what she's worth.

COACHING TIPS

- **Remove yourself from discussions about fees or prices.** Everyone in my office knows I can't be trusted to place an accurate value on my services—and stick to it. So I speak with clients about the project, scope of work, and so on, but my client services director talks about the money. Her ability to speak objectively and firmly about fees has paid for her salary many times over—and has accumulated significantly more wealth for *me*.

- **Look at the big picture.** Something I learned from a seasoned executive many years ago was that people do not pay you for your time, they pay for your expertise. That is the sum total of your experience and education. We may complain about the high fees physicians charge, but the fact is, we're paying for how they got to where they can be of help to you.

- **Build profit into every sale.** I don't care whether that sale is to your mother or your best friend. There has to be some profit in it for you. You may not want to charge a friend or family member the retail price of an item, but he or she also shouldn't expect to pay for the item at cost.

- **Don't forget cost-of-living adjustments.** Perhaps you are charging what you're worth in today's market, but that doesn't mean you will still be doing so next year if you don't raise your fees. As one entrepreneur told me, "If I don't give myself a raise, who will?"

- **Consider doing pro bono work or making a donation.** For many years I significantly reduced the fee I charged to nonprofit organizations. The "cause" was more important to me than getting rich. Some of the causes pulled on my heartstrings, and I wound up working for $10 an hour in the long run when my usual fee was $250 an hour. As a result, I soon had a booming practice of nonprofits and not enough time for my full-fee clients. Then I shifted my thinking and decided if the cause was good enough, I would do the work for no charge but there would be a limited number of spaces in my practice for those kinds of clients. Similarly, if you sell a product, you can make a donation of that product and write it off as a charitable donation.

Mistake 59

Not Charging for Your Services

I have always been taught, and learned well, to put the relationship before money. In other words, it's more important to be nice than to be rich," said one woman we spoke with. And there you have it. It's one reason why women, far more than men, have an awful time pricing their services and then actually charging people for performing them. Whether a friend asks you to tailor something for her because you're good at it, or a distant relative is always asking you to cut his hair, or a colleague consistently asks you to bring homemade cakes to company functions because it's an avocation of yours, you should be paid for your services. Part of the problem here is knowing what your value is in the marketplace, and another stems from feelings of guilt for inserting money into an existing relationship.

Just because you happen to be a stay-at-home mom who has extra time or because it's a service you perform because you actually enjoy it doesn't mean you shouldn't be paid for it. If this were true, no man would ever be paid for his evening tax preparation service or going to a job he loves.

COACHING TIPS

• **Determine what your service is worth in the market.** Do a little research. Find out how much others charge for similar services, then decide on an amount you would feel comfortable charging. Take care not to shortchange yourself. You'll only wind up resenting it even more than if you don't charge at all.

- **Develop a written fee schedule.** Once you know what you're worth and what you want to charge, prepare a sheet that outlines your fees. When someone asks you to provide a service for which you should be paid, you can say, "I'd be delighted to. Let me show you my fee schedule and you can tell me how you would like to move forward." And while I'm on the subject, be sure you update your fee schedule on a regular basis. If you charged fifty dollars per hour for a particular service three years ago, you could be shortchanging yourself today if you're still charging fifty dollars.

- **Create a home-based business around your talents.** If interest indicates you have a service others value, then consider starting your own business. This will further legitimize your services and fees. Read *Home Based Business for Dummies*, by Sarah and Paul Edwards (For Dummies, 2000). It covers everything from getting started to legal considerations to marketing ideas.

- **Consider bartering.** Men have been doing this successfully for years because they understand the implicit quid pro quo inherent to relationships. A friend of mine told me that she once dated a television personality who bartered personal endorsements, testimonials, and even appearances in exchange for concert tickets, dinners at the best restaurants, and wall-to-wall carpeting for his home. Bartering came in handy for me when I first started my business and needed some technical advice about creating fee schedules, contracts, and related matters. I was doing some coaching for a well-established consulting firm and simply asked the firm's founder if he would be willing to spend a few hours with me in exchange for coaching his executive team. At that point in my career I could never have afforded to pay his fee, but I benefited from his years of experience by giving him something he needed.

Mistake 60

Overlooking Travel Opportunities

*O*ne of the greatest perks of traveling in conjunction with your job is the opportunity to visit new places. I know from experience that all too often the most you ever see of an exotic city like Paris or Rome is conference and hotel rooms. You can take advantage of the chance to spend time in some of the most exciting cities in the world if you plan ahead and negotiate. Let's say you're going to New York for a meeting, you've never been there before, and you'd like to enjoy some of the sights. The meeting starts on Tuesday and ends on Thursday. Airlines make their money from the business traveler, which is why they charge significantly more for a ticket that doesn't have a Saturday night stay. Whereas a round-trip ticket from Minneapolis to New York could cost more than $1,000 during the week, that ticket could go down to as low as $300 with the Saturday night stay. Why not take Monday or Friday as a vacation day and ask the boss to pay for an extra two nights in a hotel in exchange for saving a few hundred dollars on airfare? You might have to change to a less expensive hotel in order to justify the savings on the airline ticket, but the inconvenience is more than worth it.

Similarly, your company may have a policy of paying for business-class airfare for travel overseas. You're going to Paris and would like to take a week's vacation there. Suggest that you fly in coach instead of business class. This results in considerable savings that could cover at least a few nights in a hotel. You get to see Paris and your employer still saves money. Of course, workload and other factors have to be considered. You definitely don't want to make the suggestion in the middle of a month-end accounting close or when your employer is about to downsize. Under the right circumstances, though, business travel offers you a great chance to live a rich life at a fraction of what it would otherwise cost.

COACHING TIPS

• **Plan your vacations around business travel.** Even if your employer isn't willing to let you trade business class for coach or doesn't see the value in saving money with the Saturday night stay, having your airfare paid for to a place you've been dying to see still adds up to a lot of savings. Yes, you may have to fork over the money for the hotel, but you're paying only half of what the trip would have cost without the airfare paid for.

• **Check out online specials.** Web sites such as Orbitz.com and Expedia.com often offer travel packages that include airfare, hotel, and sometimes even a rental car. You can save money by booking the trip as a package deal.

• **Negotiate to have a spouse or friend travel with you.** Again, for what you pay for a business-class ticket, you can often get two coach tickets. Be honest about your plan to spend vacation time in the city of destination and ask if it would be a problem to apply the cost of the higher business-class fare to two coach tickets. Smart employers will see this as an inexpensive way of keeping a good employee happy and motivated.

Mistake 61

Not Using Up Your Vacation Time

*W*hen it comes to vacation time, American workers not only get fewer days per year than their European counterparts, they also end the year with more unused days in their vacation accounts. Consider these findings from a 2003 survey conducted by Expedia.com:

- The average American leaves 1.8 days per year of his or her vacation time unused—and that means they are giving back to their employers $19.3 billion and 415 million unused days annually.
- Executives were expected to take 50 percent fewer vacation days in 2003 than they did the previous year.
- Americans are taking 10 percent less vacation time this year than they did last year.
- Nearly 50 percent of full-time workers say they are too busy to take vacations.
- Approximately 40 percent of those surveyed said they canceled or postponed vacation plans because of work.

You're probably all too familiar with why so much vacation time is left on the table. The reasons range from "I don't want to look bad to the boss" to "I know the work will only pile up, so I can't relax anyway." What you may not know is that a twenty-year study (the Framingham Heart Study) found that women who took two or more vacations a year cut their chance of a fatal heart attack in half as compared with women who took no vacation.

Living a rich life isn't about being a human *doing*, it's about taking the time to be a human *being*. My own belief is that we've all become so accustomed to living life at a breakneck speed that it's physically difficult to slow down. When the heart isn't racing and the endorphins aren't pumping, we don't feel quite alive. Sometimes we don't even know what to do with ourselves when we have "downtime." And this is a big mistake. Rest and relaxation not only contribute to your overall mental and physical health, they contribute to your portfolio as well. Taking time off gives you the opportunity to look at your life and work goals from a different perspective. When you're running at 150 mph, it's often difficult to see how you might like to do things differently. I've worked in human resources for more than twenty-five years and I would like to see vacations be not a benefit of employment, but a *requirement* of employment. Companies and employees alike reap the rewards of a refreshed and rejuvenated mind and body.

COACHING TIPS

• **Unused vacation time never makes or breaks a career.** Just because some people in your company see it as a badge of courage to end the year with unused vacation days doesn't mean you have to succumb to peer pressure. And if you're a manager, it's even more important that you be a role model for your employees by taking your own vacation time and encouraging them to do the same.

• **Take shorter, more frequent vacations.** If you're worried that your job will be gone if you take all two or three weeks of vacation time at once, take long weekends combined with Monday holidays.

• **Schedule vacations at the beginning of the year.** I've learned from experience that if I don't schedule my vacations early in the year, the year goes by and come December, I haven't taken the time off I need to be my most effective at work, in my relationships, and with the activities that are most important to me. This isn't to say you might not have to postpone vacation plans if something urgent comes up at work—but the key word here is *postpone*, not *cancel*. As soon as you know you're going to have to make a change, get another set of vacation dates on the calendar.

• **Develop a passion outside of work.** If work is your passion and you don't have things you love to do outside of the office, it's less likely you'll want to take vacation time. If you're single, you may be most vulnerable to this phenomenon—you may not have a network of friends to vacation with, you may not have hobbies that engage you, or you may find the relationships at work so rewarding that you actually would rather be in the office than home alone. Whether you're single or partnered, you've gotta have a life outside the office.

Mistake 62

Ignoring Tuition Reimbursement and Training Opportunities

*W*ith the cost of college tuition skyrocketing, you stand to save a ton of money if your employer has a tuition-reimbursement program. Even if they don't have a formal policy, some employers are willing to pay for a portion of the costs associated with helping you acquire the skills needed that would add value to the company. Although you usually can't expect a business to pay for a degree in anthropology, they may pay for some of the prerequisite classes needed to earn that degree where the skills are transferable to your job.

Many companies also have training budgets that are rarely depleted at the end of each fiscal year. If you're working so hard that you can't take time to attend a workshop, you're making a huge mistake. Instead of considering training a nicety, look at it as an investment in your future. When you go to change jobs or want to be considered for a promotion within your own company, the hiring source is going to want to know what you've done to keep up your skills in your field or develop yourself professionally to prepare for an advanced position. I remember hearing one CEO tell a group of new hires, "I'm delighted you're here; now be prepared to leave." What he meant was that the company couldn't guarantee employment for life but could offer employability for life if workers would take advantage of the many professional development opportunities offered.

A development area I know quite a bit about is executive coaching. In recent years it's become popular among not only executives but also other professionals who want to learn the nuances required to be successful and more competitive in the workplace. There are even people who specialize in "transition coaching"—helping new employees learn how to navigate through the corporate culture. The cost of a good business coach can run upwards of $300 hourly, so taking advantage of coaches that your company offers is another great way to live rich without paying for it out of your own pocket.

COACHING TIPS

• **Research companies with tuition-reimbursement programs.** If you're thinking about going back to school for your first degree or an advanced degree, it's worth spending some time finding out what companies are willing to pay for a portion of your education. H. J. Cummins, who writes for *BusinessWeek*, says that she knows of no list of companies that offer it, but that "tuition reimbursement is such a popular recruiting tool that companies are likely to bring it up even before you do. If not, it is kosher these days to ask." Here are some other considerations she suggests you be aware of:

- Four in five companies state that they offer tuition reimbursement, according to a national member-company survey for 2000 by the Society for Human Resource Management. But those are businesses big enough to have some human relations staff. Only one in three small companies offers reimbursement, says the U.S. Labor Department.
- The first $5,250 in tuition reimbursement is tax-free for undergraduate college courses (but not graduate school).

- Some companies make you repeat a course at your own expense if you fail. Others make you pay back all your tuition if you leave the company too soon—within three years, for example.
- The tight job market that's driving generous benefits is also making study sabbaticals harder to obtain. So don't expect time off. Ask for flextime instead.
- If you're lucky, some companies give stock as a graduation gift.

- **Regularly review the company's course schedule.** Many larger companies publish a schedule of training programs. Ask your human resources or training professional to put you on the distribution list for the schedule so that you don't miss what is sometimes a onetime offering.
- **Be willing to ask for training.** If you work for a smaller company or organization where training is not de rigueur, don't be afraid to ask to attend a particular training program that you believe would add value to your employer. Just because you don't know whether it will be of value to you in the future doesn't mean you should forgo the opportunity to learn in the present. Unless you know you're going to be leaving within a few weeks or months, don't be a "girl"—prepare yourself for your next job.

Mistake 63

Not Reading Nice Girls Don't Get the Corner Office: 101 Unconscious Mistakes Women Make That Sabotage Their Careers

*A*t the moment, you're reading a book about getting rich, aren't you? Well, what kind of role model would I be for you if I didn't mention my own national best seller! *Corner Office*, as I affectionately refer to it, contains the most common mistakes I've seen women make that impede their ability to achieve their career goals. These mistakes include waiting to be recognized, failure to play by the rules of the workplace, making miracles, and having no time to enjoy a life outside of work. Just as *this* book contains hundreds of tips for getting rich, that book contains hundreds of tips for how to gain credibility, confidence, and satisfaction at work—and those correlate directly with leading a rich life.

COACHING TIPS

• **Read *Nice Girls Don't Get the Corner Office*.** You can buy it from your local bookstore, order it from an online bookseller, or, if you'd like an autographed copy, you can order it from my Web site, www.drloisfrankel.com.

Chapter Eight

Playing It Smart with Your Money

The most common way people give up their power is by thinking they don't have any.

ALICE WALKER

I'm a huge believer in sharing one's wealth—whether it's a wealth of time, money, or resources. In fact, in Jewish households there's often something called a *tzedakah*—a small box into which you put money for the less fortunate. Interestingly, the word *tzedakah* is the Hebrew term for charity, and it was derived from the phrase *tzadeh-dalet kog,* meaning justice or fairness. So it's not necessarily true that you share money because you are altruistic; rather, you feel it's the right or just thing to do—share your wealth. But women often take this notion to the extreme—a *far* extreme. And we do it in ways that on the surface seem logical, kind, and nurturing. Of course! We were once little girls who were taught to be this way.

A client of mine recently told me that while driving to work one day, she was practicing envisioning more abundance in her life. Immediately after she pictured this, she got out of her car and spotted two dollars lying in the parking lot outside her office. Feeling good about her find, she walked into the lobby of her building and gave one dollar to the receptionist. When I asked why she did this, she said it was "found" money and it made her feel good, so she wanted to share the good feeling. It made me curious to know what a man would have done in the same situation, so I conducted a (not so scientific) survey and asked ten men how they would have responded to finding the money. Most of the men said it would never occur to them to give any part of it away, although they might use it to buy a friend a beer.

However you choose to spend, lend, share, invest, or give away your money is up to you—but allowing others to take advantage of your generosity and not advocating for yourself isn't smart. This chapter focuses on the myriad ways in which women sabotage themselves from getting rich because they feel compelled to give away time or money. Bear in mind I'm not saying there's no place for altruism, philanthropy, or loss leaders—but it's a lot smarter to act *consciously*.

Mistake 64

Failure to Negotiate

*T*here is so much information written in books and articles about women and negotiation that I'm not going to spend a lot of time on this subject. With that said, I do want to mention a must-read book titled *Women Don't Ask: Negotiation and the Gender Divide* (Princeton University Press, 2003). Authors Linda Babcock and Sara Laschever have done a remarkable job of describing the fears and factors that impede women from getting what they want—whether it's a fair price on a car, the help they need to do the job effectively, or the bonus that they earned. Their research shows that women exhibit "considerably more apprehension" when it comes to negotiation than men.

In one part of an extensive survey the authors asked women and men to describe how they thought about negotiation. Results revealed that "men associated words such as *exciting* and *fun* with negotiation far more than women, who were more likely to use words like *scary*." When one of the authors asked her students why they enrolled in her negotiation-skills class, men were more likely to reply that they wanted to improve their skills, whereas women reported that they wanted to learn to overcome their discomfort with negotiation. Their bottom line is simple: Women don't get as much as men because they don't ask for it, and they don't ask because negotiations make them anxious.

COACHING TIPS

- **Read** *The Shadow Negotiation: How Women Can Master the Hidden Agendas That Determine Bargaining Success.* I routinely recommend this book by Deborah Kolb and Judith Williams (Simon & Schuster, 2000) to women clients. What I like about it is that it focuses on how women think about negotiation and the most common stumbling blocks that women encounter when they try to negotiate for what is rightfully theirs.
- **Prepare for every negotiation.** It doesn't matter if you're negotiating with your boss for a raise, with a salesperson for a car, or with your fiancé over the place to hold your wedding reception, preparation is the key to success when it comes to increasing the likelihood that your needs will be met (at best) or considered (at least) in negotiation outcomes. Here are five tips to get you started with preparing to negotiate:

  - Focus on outcomes. What is it that you want to walk away with? If it's a raise, how much do you want? If you're buying a car, how much are you willing to pay? Being as specific as possible also increases the likelihood of negotiation success.
  - Before entering into a negotiation, prepare yourself with data, facts, and figures. In other words, support your desired outcome with data that point to its reasonableness.
  - A negotiation is not the time to "wing it." Writing down your key points in advance—and practicing them—enables you to stay focused on what's most important and avoid going off on tangents.
  - Err on the side of asking for more, rather than less. It's been shown that people who enter into negotiations

asking for more than what they want are likely to walk away with *at least* what they want—and sometimes more.

- Be willing to walk away. If you know the parameters of your expectations (i.e., the lower and upper ends of what you're willing to pay or accept), then you'll know when to do so. In the long run it's rarely worth it to pay more or accept less than you expect.

- **Take a class on negotiation.** There are so many factors that go into being a good negotiator that you can't be expected to know them intuitively. Negotiation classes and workshops provide you with the language and tips that contribute to enhancing your skill and comfort in the negotiation process. Start by going to the Web site www.theshadownegotiation.com. Here you'll find a series of online interactive programs designed for women by the authors of *The Shadow Negotiation*.

Mistake 65

Loaning Money to Family and Friends

*W*e heard many stories from the women we interviewed about making the mistake of loaning money to friends or family and actually thinking they would get it back. As one woman from Cleveland told me, "When you loan money to friends or family members, you should just consider it a gift." She's right. Whereas you might think you're doing the right thing by loaning money, you may actually be setting yourself up to lose that relationship in the long run. Of course, there are several factors to consider, such as the amount of the loan, your relationship with this person, the person's past history of repaying loans, and the need for the loan. Making a conscious choice about loaning money means understanding the difference between loaning money so the person can have some kind of critical surgery and loaning money so that the person can pay off his or her credit card debt.

Nicole, a woman I met on the North Slope of Alaska, provides just one example of the horror stories that relate to loaning money to friends. During a training session break I asked her why she thought she wasn't rich. Without missing a beat, Nicole said it was because she loaned a large amount of money to a friend who was divorced with two children. The money was intended to help the friend get on her feet and through a difficult financial period. She later found out that her friend was living with an unemployed boyfriend and *his* three children, and the money was actually going to support all of them. Here Nicole was, working in a remote location away from her own children for two weeks at a time, and her friend was living comfortably (and unemployed) off of her money. Needless to say, she felt as if she was sucker punched.

COACHING TIPS

• **Before you loan money, probe deeply into what the money is going to be used for.** It's not a crime to know where your money is going to go. If you think it's not a good enough cause to loan your money to, say so.

• **Consider the reason why you would agree to loan the money.** If it's because you have a hard time saying no or because you feel bad for the person, think again. Don't let your need to be liked interfere with your need to be financially independent.

• **Negotiate.** Just because someone asks for a loan of $5,000 doesn't mean you have to give it. Under certain circumstances you might be willing to loan $500 but not $5,000. Set limits on the amount you're willing to potentially lose.

• **Consider the person's history of repayment.** If you've loaned this person money in the past and haven't gotten it back, don't be stupid. No matter what his or her promises or appeals, you're not going to get this loan back either.

• **Get it in writing.** When you loan a significant amount of money, have the person sign a loan document. It may cause the person to think twice about borrowing the money in the first place, and it increases the likelihood of getting the money back. The document doesn't necessarily have to be formal, but it should include the person's name, the loan amount, and any agreements about a repayment schedule. If the person balks at the idea of signing something or makes you feel guilty about even suggesting it, walk away. Anyone who is asking for part of your wealth should be willing to commit to repaying it.

• **Don't loan what you can't lose.** Think about how you would feel or what kind of financial condition you would be in if the loan wasn't repaid. If you can't afford to lose it, don't loan it. This rule of thumb also prevents you from losing a friend or important relationship. It may be better to have the person angry with you for a short period of time than to lose the relationship permanently.

- **Make a predated check a contingency for a loan.** When you loan money, do so with the proviso that the person write you a check for the amount he or she agrees to pay back, dated for some agreed-upon time in the future.

Mistake 66

Giving Away Money

*L*oaning money is one thing. Giving it away is another. Consider these mistakes made by some of the women in our survey:

I gave away to all my friends, particularly boyfriends, my entire silver dollar collection, which had been given to me over many years by a great-aunt. I could have all those pure silver dollars today had I not given them away in an effort to make people like me.

I gave my ex-husband money to start a business without any real discussion. No wonder he's my ex.

I told my parents to keep the amount of money I was going to inherit in their wills. They wanted to give me three-quarters of the money and my brother one-quarter, but in my quest to be independent I talked them out of it.

I gave my ex-husband $100 right after he left me for the babysitter because he had run out of money and I felt sorry for him.

I once dated a guy who never had any money because he had huge child support payments. I ended up paying most of the dating costs, and the situation just made me feel very used and unhappy.

What each of these mistakes has in common is that they were made from the heart, not the head. When it comes to choosing between a relationship or giving money away, the former wins out almost every time. Faced with the question of whether to prepare for their financial futures or share their money with loved ones, it's no competition. Women want those they care about to have what they want and will sacrifice their own well-being for the needs of others. It's all part of the "nice girl" syndrome. Selflessly doing for others can not only impede you from having the financial freedom you've dreamed of, it can actually contribute to your ultimately having less than you need to live adequately, let alone well.

COACHING TIPS

- **Plan your financial gift giving.** A few hundred here or a few thousand there may not seem like a lot to you, but over time it adds up. Have a budget for what you are willing to give away and stick with it. It can be a yearly budget or an amount that you give away upon inheriting money. Consider giving everyone whom you might give money to during the year his or her share at one time. Make it clear, however, that it's a onetime gift and there's no coming back to drink from the trough.
- **Offer alternatives to financial support.** If someone you care about is starting a business, going through a tough time, or needs money for some other reason (legitimate or otherwise), offering or agreeing to give them money isn't the only way you can show your support. Here are a few things to consider in lieu of giving money:

  - Help them complete the paperwork to apply for a loan.
  - Babysit while they go on interviews.

- Provide information on resources for which they would be eligible.
- Assist them with updating a résumé, doing a budget, practicing for an interview or loan negotiation.
- Give them the names of people in your own network who could be of help, such as a lawyer, CPA, or bank officer.
- Offer sanctuary in the form of dinner, a seminar, or a movie.

- **Separate money from friendship or love.** Anyone who truly loves you or who wants to be your friend won't require money to show it. If they do, a huge red flag should go up as a warning that you're about to enter dangerous territory.
- **Just say no.** Yes, I know it's hard. Yes, I understand it goes against everything you believe in. Yes, I realize you just want to share what you have. But you'll never become financially independent if you keep giving your money away. After the first few times, saying no gets easier—so start practicing now.

Mistake 67

Not Advocating for Yourself During a Divorce or Separation from a Life or Business Partner

*E*ven though they had been going to couples counseling for several months, Joan was shocked when her husband came home one day and asked for a divorce. She knew they had problems but hoped they could work things out. What she didn't know at the time was that her husband was having an affair with a woman in his office and that the likelihood of making this marriage work was a long shot. His pronouncement, and the fact that he had already found long-term housing in a hotel and immediately began moving his things out of their home, put Joan into a deep depression. She could barely get out of bed in the morning, let alone handle her husband's demands to make this divorce happen, and happen fast.

Joan made several of the worst mistakes possible when it came to advocating for herself and her two teenage girls— both before and after divorce proceedings were under way. To begin with, her husband, a CFO for a *Fortune* 100 company, handled all the finances and investments. She had no idea what their portfolio looked like. Next, being conflict-averse, Joan didn't want to enter into an adversarial divorce, and so when her husband suggested they just allow the family attorney to handle the paperwork involved, she went along with it. And even when it looked like he was not going to treat her fairly, she failed to seek advice or representation for herself.

Joan's reaction isn't unlike that of many women who are

faced with an unexpected or unwanted divorce or separation. It is often emotionally devastating and can make you question your self-worth, diminish your self-confidence, and damage your self-esteem. Combined, these factors might make you want to avoid the logistics required to separate property and income. By so doing, however, not only do you wind up giving away more valuable resources than you should, but you give away your power as well.

COACHING TIPS

- **Expect the best, prepare for the worst.** It might be nice to think that your spouse or partner will treat you fairly, but don't count on it. If he or she has legal representation, then you need it too. And don't fall for the line "Why don't we use the same person—it will be cheaper in the long run." It's difficult for one person to represent two people equitably; inevitably, the professional's own feelings, experiences, or biases come into play.

- **Don't acquiesce to the other person's sense of urgency.** So your husband finds this woman half your age whom he wants to make his trophy wife. He might want to make the divorce process a "quickie," but you don't have to go along with it. When in doubt, rent the movie *The First Wives Club*. Although there's no need to drag out a divorce for an interminable period of time out of spite (why subject yourself, your family, and your friends to the misery?), there's also no rule that says it has to be entirely on the other person's terms.

- **Ask for documentation.** I once knew a woman who let her husband handle all the family finances. When they decided to divorce, she wanted to make it an amicable parting of the ways, in large part for the sake of their children. At first she trusted everything he said. But when he said his busy dental practice (the same one that kept him away from home working sixty hours or more each week) was yielding only $35,000 in annual income, she took off the gloves. Tax records showed he was paying tax on significantly more than $35,000 and had stashed away a huge amount in savings and profit sharing.

- **Get psychological help.** A divorce or separation is one of the most traumatic relationship experiences you will go through. It's not the time to be stoic. Getting help from a mental health professional can assist you with developing the emotional stamina needed to get through the challenges you will face.

Writing for Divorcemagazine.com, Nancy Kurn, director of Educational Services for the Institute for Divorce Financial Analysts (IDFA), gives these additional tips for how to avoid a financial disaster during a divorce:

- **Negotiate a reasonable settlement.** Get some professional advice from a certified divorce financial analyst (CDFA) or certified financial planner (CFP) to make sure you'll be able to live with the financial terms of the settlement—now and into the future.
- **Don't live beyond your income.** Reduce your expenses—or increase your income—so that you are always saving something for a rainy day. If necessary, ask your financial adviser for help in creating a budget.
- **Think twice about keeping the family home.** Ask your financial adviser whether you can truly afford it and ask him or her to show you what cash you'd have available for investment if you moved to a smaller home.

- **Realize that you won't get everything you want in the property division.** Don't spend months and thousands of dollars fighting over furniture, appliances, or other personal items. Make a short list of "must-haves" and be prepared to compromise on everything else. Look at the big picture: Is this asset best for your situation?

- **Use debt sparingly.** Get a copy of your credit report and close all joint accounts and all credit you do not use. Avoid maintaining balances on credit cards.

- **Get the information you need before making any commitments.** Will you need to go back to school so that you can resume your career? While you were married, did you earn your Ph.T. (Putting Hubby Through) by paying for his law school or medical school and you are now entitled to remuneration for this? These are just two examples of things to be considered *before* you sign on the dotted line. For more information about how a CDFA can help you, visit IDFA's Web site at www.institutedfa.com or call 800-875-1760.

Mistake 68

Being Insurance-Poor

*L*ife insurance, disability insurance, car insurance, long-term-care insurance, health insurance, property insurance, travel insurance, earthquake insurance—and the list goes on. It's enough to make a sane woman crazy trying to figure out which ones are must-haves and which would be nice to have. Then, once you decide on the type of insurance to purchase, how much do you want it to cover? All of your out-of-pocket expenses? Anything over $1,000? Author and financial adviser Ginita Wall reminds us that too many people live by the insurance agents' motto: "If you can afford the insurance you have, then you don't have enough."

Let me be clear. Being *properly* insured is important. Being *overly* insured is foolish. Too many of us have become fearful of not having enough insurance—regardless of the kind. It's a waste of money to be overinsured. That's money you can be using for a down payment on a home, putting into retirement, or paying for your child's college education. Being under-insured, however, is dangerous. We've all heard stories about people who have no health insurance, get into a catastrophic car wreck, and are left with a lifetime of medical bills to pay. The proper balance between the kinds of insurance you elect to purchase and the amount of insurance you opt for in each policy is something you should take time to think through. Just because some insurance salesperson says you need this policy or that deductible doesn't make it true. As with all of your other purchases, do the research, consider your priorities, and make a decision that meets the needs of you and your family.

COACHING TIPS

- **Consider the facts before buying insurance.** The type of insurance you buy and how much coverage you select depend on your individual situation. Some factors to consider:

  - Do you have dependents? If not, there are very few reasons why you would need life insurance. Although a variety of factors contribute to determining how much life insurance is prudent for your situation, one rule of thumb is that at a minimum you should be insured for your current household income multiplied by 7. If you and your spouse earn a total of $90,000 annually, that would amount to $630,000 in life insurance ($90,000 x 7).
  - Do you or your family depend on your income for survival? If so, disability insurance is probably a wise buy. At almost any age you are five to six times more likely to become disabled than die.
  - How much can you afford for out-of-pocket expenses? If you can afford the first $2,000 for any claim, be it for a car accident or medical costs, then why pay for a low deductible? You can save thousands of dollars over the course of your life and not be any the worse for it.
  - Health insurance is always in fashion. We've all heard horror stories of the person who gets sick, has no insurance, and winds up with a lifetime of medical bills to pay.

- **Only buy from a stable insurer.** You can be fooled by rock-bottom insurance prices only to find when you need it most that the company is out of business. Before buying from any company, check them out on A. M. Best's Worldwide Insurance Directory at www.ambest.com.

- **Comparison shop.** Like everything else, insurance prices vary from provider to provider. When I bought a new home several years ago, I assumed the big-name insurers would be more costly and didn't even bother checking into them for homeowners' insurance. After the Northridge earthquake in California, a friend told me how well State Farm took care of the significant amount of damage she incurred, so I looked into them. It turned out they were far more reasonable than I'd thought, and I knew I could count on them, so I switched from my "no name" carrier.

Mistake 69

Not Maximizing Legitimate Tax Deductions

$\mathcal{D}$id you know there are actually two kinds of money? Pretax and posttax dollars are not the same thing. Your goal is to minimize pretax dollars and maximize posttax dollars. What's the difference? You can't spend all of the money you earn before you pay tax on it because a certain percentage will ultimately go to the government. By reducing the amount that is taxable, you keep more in your pocket to spend or invest.

The Internal Revenue Service has instilled fear in the hearts of many Americans to the point where they are reluctant to take advantage of even legitimate tax-saving measures. Being overly cautious when it comes to preparing your tax returns is tantamount to giving away your money to the government. Don't you give them enough money in income, sales, and property taxes? Do you really need to be giving them more?

Consider these frequently overlooked deductions that can save you thousands of dollars in taxes:

- Medical care for dependent parents
- Transportation costs when receiving medical care
- Charitable donations
- Annual gift exclusion
- Lifetime Learning Credit
- Job hunting expenses

Of course, you should always research the requirements of any deduction to determine whether or not you are eligible for it, but taking the time to do so is well worth it.

COACHING TIPS

- **If you do your own tax preparation, invest in TurboTax or other software.** These programs make preparing your own taxes easy and reduce the likelihood of mistakes in calculation. For as little as $39 you can save hours poring over the paperwork required to complete your return.
- **Keep good records throughout the year.** Whether you prepare your own tax returns or have them professionally prepared, save receipts, request acknowledgment letters for items that you donate (cash or goods), and make notations about other potentially tax-deductible expenditures. If you think on February 10 of one year that you'll remember what you spent for tax preparation purposes the next year, think again. You'll lose out on hundreds of dollars' worth of deductions by not keeping track as you go along.
- **Use the _Ernst & Young Tax Guide_ as a reference.** There are many tax guides available, but I like this one because it's comprehensive (more than seven hundred information-packed pages), relatively easy to read, and written by people who really know taxes.
- **Get professional advice.** The more complex your financial situation, the wiser it is to seek professional help when preparing your returns. Even if you don't want to have someone else prepare them for you, by paying for a consultation you can take advantage of the professional's knowledge and expertise.

Mistake 70

Enabling Adult Children to Lead Unrealistic Lifestyles

*N*early every financial planner I spoke with as I conducted research for this book mentioned this as one of the biggest mistakes a woman makes later in her financial life. Whether it's giving their children money to send the grandkids to private schools or housing their children long after they should be independent, women are more likely than men to give up their financial security because of the misguided belief that they should be supplementing their adult children's incomes. Not only does this largesse deplete the woman's retirement savings typically at the time she needs it most, it doesn't benefit her children. It increases the child's sense of entitlement and decreases the sense of responsibility for having to live within one's means.

One financial planner shared with me the story of one of her clients, a retired woman living from the funds contained in a trust. The planner noticed that the woman was taking large amounts of money from the trust to the point where within five years the trust would contain less than the amount she needed to live. As they discussed it, she learned that the money being taken out of the trust was not being used by her client, but rather being given to the client's daughter to pay for private school for her own child to the tune of $20,000 annually. Now, if money is no object for you and giving it to your kids for cars, houses, or private schools in no way impedes your ability to live the lifestyle you want, by all means give it away. But if you're anything like most women, the following coaching tips will be of help.

COACHING TIPS

- **Express the desire to remain financially independent.** When your kids come to you with hands held out for money, learn to say, "The best gift I can give you is for me to be financially secure and not be a burden to you in my old age."

- **Use your investment adviser as the "bad guy."** It was an investment adviser who suggested this. She recommends that her clients tell their children, "Let me check first with my investment adviser." You can then go back and say, "I'm so sorry. My investment adviser says I can't afford to do that."

- **Teach kids fiscal responsibility.** People do run into difficult spots, and helping out from time to time (if you can afford it) isn't such a bad thing. In fact, you can give unlimited money for medical or educational expenses without being limited by the $11,000 annual gift exclusion. But paying for a nanny or private school when your kids can't afford it is not a good idea. By refusing to underwrite unnecessary expenditures, you give your children the satisfaction of making their way in the world—a lesson they may not *want* to learn, but one that they do need to learn.

Mistake 71

Underestimating or Ignoring the Value of Your Assets

*A*lthough she laughs about it now, when one woman considered the financial mistakes she made in her life, she counted as the worst the time she spent her father's "entire collection of silver dollars dating from 1800 to 1900 on bologna sandwiches." During college when she was broke she took one bologna sandwich a day to school with her. Another woman told us about inheriting her mother's collection of jewelry. Given the fact that she and her mother had very different tastes, she couldn't imagine wearing any of it and thought most of it was costume jewelry with little or no value. So she gave it to (of all people) her former mother-in-law, who had often admired her mother's jewelry. She later came to find out there were several very valuable pieces worth in excess of $10,000. And to answer what you must be wondering—no, her former mother-in-law had no intention of returning the jewelry or sharing the wealth.

Many times you acquire through purchase, settlement, or inheritance items you later decide you don't like or don't particularly value. It may be because you don't like them, because they're a painful reminder of someone you'd rather forget, or because you have no clue as to what they're really worth. If you've ever watched PBS's *Antiques Roadshow*, you know that one person's trash is literally another person's treasure.

COACHING TIPS

- **If you're not sure of the value of goods, have them assessed.** You can find appraisers of various types of collectibles at the *Antiques Roadshow* Web site, www.pbs.org/wgbh/pages/roadshow. It's not a bad idea to get several appraisals, particularly if you're thinking of selling the item to the appraiser.

- **Search the value of collectibles on eBay.** This is a good place to start a search to get a ballpark idea of the value others are attaching to the same items.

- **Hold on to it for a little while longer.** If you have an emotional reason for wanting to get rid of something (like it reminds you of your former mother-in-law, whom you couldn't stand), hold on to it for a little while and see if you don't change your mind. It could be that once the emotions subside, you will be better able to make an informed decision.

- **Search for "lost" money.** Remember that company you worked for when you were eighteen and in college? Are you entitled to a pension that you either didn't know about or forgot about? Or how about eccentric Aunt Millie, who stashed money everywhere but died with no will? Maybe she had a few bank accounts that no one even knew about. Check out www.pbgc.gov/search to find out whether your name is on the rolls of any pension plans in their database. Another site, www.unclaimed.org, can direct you to the state Web sites charged with uniting legitimate heirs with unclaimed property and funds.

Mistake 72

Succumbing to Sales Pressure

$\mathscr{I}$ put this mistake into this particular section because when you can't say no to a salesperson or the kid who comes to your door selling magazine subscriptions you really don't want, it's the same as giving away your money. Women are far more likely to make this mistake than men. The Do Not Call Registry is the best thing our legislators have done for us in a long time. Too many women were easy marks for unscrupulous telephone solicitors who convinced you that you really won a "free" trip to Hawaii (for a small cost) or bilked you into contributing to some worthy cause that didn't even exist. If men don't want something, they walk away, close the door, or hang up the phone. As for us women, we don't want to hurt anyone's feelings, we don't want to seem impolite, or, worse yet, we don't want anyone to think poorly of us. So we give away our money to people who make us feel guilty about not buying their services or products.

It's a particularly slippery slope when purchasing an automobile. Yes, I realize car salesmen (and they are mostly men) get a bad rap and are the butt of many jokes. But you know, there's often a kernel of truth in any stereotype. You almost see the salesperson salivate when a woman walks through the door. I once went so far as to call a showroom in advance and ask if I could speak with a woman salesperson. The male on the other end of the phone hung up. A car and a home are two of the biggest investments you make during your lifetime. Don't let anyone spoil the joy and the decision by pressuring you into something that's not right for you.

COACHING TIPS

- **Register on the National Do Not Call list.** It's easy to register online (it only takes about three minutes) at www.donotcall.gov or call 888-382-1222. Once you've been registered for three months, telemarketers should not be calling your home. If they do, you can file a complaint at the same Web site or phone number where you registered.

- **Develop and practice your "no thank you" comeback line.** Saying no doesn't have to be a painful experience for you or the person to whom you're saying it. In fact, you can kill 'em with kindness. My own line is, "Thank you very much for your time [or the offer], I'm not interested." If they persist, be a broken record: "As I said, I appreciate the offer, but I won't be taking advantage of it." If they still persist, simply walk away, close the door, or hang up the phone—you've done your best to treat them with dignity (after all, they're just doing their jobs).

- **Consider using a car broker.** The process of buying or leasing a new car has been considerably more pleasant, and less expensive, since I started using a local car broker who was recommended to me by a friend. The way it works is this: You call the broker and tell him what kind of car you're looking for (it helps if you did your own research first as to prices), and he actually locates it at the best price possible and charges you a fixed service fee. You can even ask him to set up an appointment with a car dealership for you to test-drive the car. This way, you don't have salespeople pressuring you to buy. The payoff for the salesperson is the knowledge that although you won't be buying from him, the broker you are working with will—either for this purchase or at some point in the future.

Mistake 73

Not Giving Smartly

*W*hen you think of the world's most famous philanthropists, men often come to mind: John D. Rockefeller, Andrew Carnegie, Henry Ford, Bill Gates, and Ted Turner, to name a few. But women are becoming increasingly prominent in the world of philanthropy—especially women who have earned (not inherited) their wealth. Gloria Steinem and Marlo Thomas led the way when they started the Ms. Foundation for Women. You may not yet be in the category of a Rockefeller, but not planning how you give, whether it's $10 or $1,000, can prevent you from maintaining and growing your wealth so that you can make an even greater difference. The question is, if you are charitable, are you efficiently charitable? The remainder of mistakes in this chapter focus on how you can give from the heart and avoid the pitfalls often associated with charitable giving. I thank Joe Lumarda, executive vice president of the California Community Foundation in Los Angeles, for his significant contributions to this chapter.

"I know women who write twenty to thirty checks at the end of the year to all their favorite charities," says Lumarda, "but have many assets they could use in a more tax-advantageous manner. For example, if you own appreciated securities and real estate, these could be donated. Or if you're working with a sophisticated nonprofit organization, you may be able to consider gifts of limited partnership interests, shares of a closely held (private) company, personal property (such as art or other collectibles), or intellectual property (like royalties or movie rights)."

The best attitude to have when you're bit by the charitable bug is to be as creative as possible in your giving. The nonprofit sector always needs cash but will often take (and sell) whatever is availed to it.

COACHING TIPS

• **Take an inventory of your assets.** To make the smartest choice about what asset to use to fund your charitable activity, you need to know what you have. Only when you (and your advisers) know the range and choices available within your estate can you give smartly.

• **Work with your accountant (or seek a second opinion).** This is tricky. You may have an accountant who is technically very capable but not very creative. Lumarda says he has seen cases where accountants have killed perfectly good gifts because they weren't "comfortable with this." That's when you might choose to work with accountants or tax attorneys who specialize in the nonprofit sector. Sophisticated nonprofit organizations (the development or advancement departments of colleges, universities, or community foundations) in your area usually have a list of these individuals for your consideration.

• **Make sure your gift is appropriate for your nonprofit's needs.** Many nonprofit organizations are comfortable receiving assets other than cash; some are not. Have a full discussion with the executive director or development director of your charity to make sure they have the willingness—and wherewithal—to explore and execute different and creative gifts.

• **Take advantage of matching company contributions to charitable organizations.** One way to save on taxes is by making charitable donations. You can maximize your gift giving by checking with your human resources department to see if your company offers matching contributions. Many companies will match what you give dollar for dollar up to a certain amount. It's a win-win for everyone—your charity gets more, and you and your employer have a tax write-off.

Mistake 74

Starting a Nonprofit Venture without Doing Your Homework

*W*ith women increasingly going into businesses of their own, this is a trap that often leads to their undoing. The media report on women starting new nonprofit ventures for noble causes such as breast cancer, domestic violence, or public school reform all the time. What we don't hear about are the countless new nonprofit ventures that begin with enthusiasm and flourish, but end with disappointment, or worse— disappointed donors wondering where their contributions went.

Successful women who are entrepreneurs or business leaders often want to tackle social problems with the same energy and "go it alone" attitude that helped them throughout their career. Unfortunately, tackling community problems takes the same time and attention as starting a new business or running a division of a company—sometimes even more. Often, women passionate about a particular issue but not necessarily experienced in the nonprofit sector will quickly incorporate an organization, begin raising money, and apply the funds to new programs. What frequently follows is an unfortunate cycle of not having enough time to do the nonprofit venture well, while keeping on top of the moneymaking business (your day job).

This particular phenomenon happens quite a bit in the entertainment industry. Women celebrities are often led down this path by advisers who say, "No one can bring as much attention to this issue as you" and "No other nonprofit is addressing this issue quite the way we plan to." Red flags should start waving if you start to hear sentiments like this from friends (or yourself).

COACHING TIPS

• **Get smart on the issue.** When you follow your passion on an issue, don't only read the current best seller on the subject, or listen solely to the recognized guru. Think of it as if you were starting a business. If you were going into a market, the first question you would ask is, "Who is your customer?" In order to get smart on any particular issue, you may wish to call your local community foundation, United Way, or volunteer center. Remember to take your time and be patient. It sometimes takes a little while to find the right organization or person to talk to.

• **Find an organization and lend your expertise.** Ideally, you would find one or two organizations that appeal to you. Visit them. Ask for a tour. Check out their Web sites. You can even see their tax returns (look on www.guidestar.org). When you find an organization, lend some of your time utilizing your natural gifts. I would recommend you gain experience on both the programmatic side (client service—tutoring, mentoring, tree planting, etc.) and the governance side (becoming a board member) in order to get a well-balanced view of nonprofit operations.

• **Be an investor, not a donor.** When you begin this journey toward a deeper relationship with a nonprofit organization, you will be aware of and care more about the importance of your monetary contribution. With the scandals in the nonprofit sector over the past several years, there is an increased demand for public disclosure and transparency. You should know how every penny of your contribution is being used, and help the organization know the importance of this disclosure.

Mistake 75

Starting a Foundation (All My Friends Have One) without the Facts

*O*kay. Let's say you've followed all the tips in this book and now you're rich. At a cocktail party you talk to similarly successful women, and most of them mention the creation of their own private foundation. You like the sound of that. It sounds like one's made it when she has her own foundation. You call your lawyer and he says he can set one up in a jiffy. Sound good? Maybe, maybe not.

Over the years the private foundation has become somewhat of a status symbol. If your checks are going out under the name of The [Your Name Here] Foundation, it smells of success. What many people don't know is that this vehicle is a new entity, a new corporation, with its own unique and somewhat complex set of legal and accounting guidelines. And because some people have abused the privilege of establishing a private foundation, Congress, the IRS, and the attorneys general of most states have increased their scrutiny of these foundations. "The abuses include paying exorbitant fees and salaries to relatives and board members (in some cases more than the amount distributed in grants) and self-dealing (when the foundation gives preferential treatment to family and board members regarding the management and disposition of foundation assets)," says Joe Lumarda.

Don't let this discourage you, though. If you want to establish a charitable legacy, there are many options to explore. You just need to know the right places to go and people to ask.

COACHING TIPS

• **Check with an expert.** The main problem arises when a person has an idea of creating some type of foundation and goes to any attorney or adviser at the Chamber of Commerce mixer and mentions this. The adviser then says, "Sure, I can set that up for you." But as I heard a friend in this world say, "Foundations are like babies. It's a lot easier (and more pleasurable) to create one than to maintain one." There are specialists who responsibly create these types of entities. The most common adviser to go to would be an attorney with a specialty in tax-exempt organizations. They should be able to ask all the appropriate questions and create the most appropriate vehicle to facilitate your philanthropy.

• **Ask about options.** A good adviser should give you a range of options and not focus only on the creation of a private foundation. These would include donor-advised funds (usually offered by nonprofit community foundations or for-profit mutual fund companies and other financial institutions).

• **Be mindful of ongoing operations and succession.** Much like a new (or old) business, issues of regulations, operations, and succession should be considered when creating a private foundation. Beware if an adviser establishes a foundation for you without addressing these issues.

• **Know you have resources.** There are national and local trade associations of foundations. One national organization is the Council on Foundations, www.cof.org. It provides counsel and support to foundations in all phases of development and operation.

Chapter Nine

Resources

I myself have never been able to find out precisely what feminism is: I only know that people call me a feminist whenever I express sentiments that differentiate me from a doormat.

REBECCA WEST, 1913

Throughout this book I've mentioned Web sites, books, and other resources that could be helpful to you as you begin developing your personal game plan for getting rich. As a convenience for you, I've listed all of them here—along with several others that may not have fit into the chapters and mistakes, but which are nonetheless valuable sources of information for you. As with any resource, you have to use your own best judgment as to how well they suit your needs. A suggestion from one person or place that works for your best friend may not work for you. With this in mind, consider where you want to start learning more about how to lead the life you want—and deserve.

SELECTING AN INVESTMENT ADVISER

Finding the right financial adviser is a little like finding the right therapist or even life partner. You try a few out, you make some mistakes, and when you find the right one, you know it. Don't be surprised if you go through several before locating a person you trust, one who will listen to you and with whom you can have a long-term relationship. The following "five Ps" are provided courtesy of Chartered Financial Analyst Institute for use in conjunction with finding the adviser who is right for you.

- **Preparation.** Before you even start looking for an investment adviser, research investor publications for information on choosing the right investment goals for your lifestyle. With this knowledge, prepare a list of questions to ask the people you interview. Similarly, ask yourself what kind of adviser you want. Is it someone who will partner with you in managing your investments, or do you want to give that person control over making decisions about your portfolio? Ask friends for referrals, and research the background of the adviser before making a final decision.
- **Professionalism.** Your investment adviser will have access to the most intimate details of your finances, so trust is important. Most advisers will be willing to have an introductory meeting with you at no cost. Such meetings provide you with the opportunity to decide how comfortable you are with the person both personally and professionally. Many investment firms have standards of ethics that exceed those required by federal regulations. Ask whether such standards exist in an adviser's organization and how they are administered and whether you will be informed if he or she becomes the subject of an ethical or regulatory investigation when you are working together. Don't be intimidated by jargon or buzzwords used by the adviser. Ask for an explanation of terms you don't understand.
- **Philosophy.** Asking questions about an adviser's invest-

ment philosophy is one of the most important steps in choosing an adviser who can help you achieve your personal investment goals. Is the adviser conservative or aggressive with regard to his or her investment philosophy? If the adviser works for an investment firm, ask to see information on the firm's philosophy as well. The size of an investment organization is not necessarily an indication of the adviser's ability. Find out whether the adviser's philosophy would be influenced by corporate or management changes. Find out how often the adviser will communicate with you and in what format (i.e., meeting, writing, phone).

• **Performance.** Analyzing performance results is another important aspect of selecting an investment adviser. Be aware that there are many considerations in determining performance, including the investment instruments utilized and market activity. Compare the adviser's performance with leading benchmarks such as Standard & Poor's 500. Also find out how the adviser is paid. Determine whether an adviser's performance data include the impact of fees charged to clients and whether he or she receives compensation from anyone other than clients.

• **Professional designations.** Financial professionals may hold one or more designations that represent their competence in specific areas of their profession. For example, someone with the designation CFA (chartered financial adviser) has completed a three-year program that covers the fundamentals underlying investment theory. They tend to have a more quantitative understanding of the dynamics of investing. A CFP (certified financial planner), on the other hand, has studied for a more practical approach to investment and may focus on a wider range of issues related to tax, insurance, and other areas. This person works more with the client on making the right choices about the options available. One isn't better than the other, and both indicate that the person has taken the time, energy, and money needed to become an expert in the field. To learn more about the requirements of each designation, go online to www.nasd.com/investor/resources/designations. You can also verify an adviser's designation through the following sources:

- Chartered financial analyst (CFA), 800-247-8132
- Chartered investment counselor (CIC), 202-293-4222
- Certified financial planner (CFP), www.cfp.net/search
- Chartered financial consultant (ChFC), www.financialpro. org/consumer/referral.cfm
- Certified public accountant (CPA) or personal financial specialist (PFS), www.aicpa.org/accredrefweb/pfssearch.asp

Three other Web sites that are definitely worth checking out in your search for the right investment adviser are:

- **CFA Institute**
  www.cfainstitute.org
  This association of financial professionals was founded for the purpose of educating the public and its members as well as identifying the standards of ethics related to the investment field. Their investor services section contains information about how to know if you need a financial adviser, the different types of advisers available, common mistakes advisers make, and how to manage a relationship with a financial adviser. You can also use the site to help locate a member in your area.

- **Investment Counsel Association of America**
  www.icaa.org

ICAA is similar to CFA Institute, but its members tend to work with investors with portfolios in excess of $250,000. The site has a listing of members by region to help you identify an adviser in your area.

- **National Association of Personal Financial Advisors www.napfa.org**
  This organization can give you names of members in your area who work for a fee rather than commissions.

Finally, when it comes to selecting an investment adviser, consider these commonsense tips:

- **Ask questions.** Women are often reluctant to ask questions because they don't want to put someone on the spot or appear as if they don't trust the person. This is just another way the "nice girl" tape plays in our heads and trips us up. If someone is insulted because you're asking questions about how he or she suggests you invest your money, you should take it as a sign this isn't someone you can trust—and don't feel guilty about it either!
- **Ask for referrals.** Picking an investment adviser or planning firm from the yellow pages isn't a great idea. Your best source for referrals is from people who have firsthand knowledge of investment professionals and have seen positive results from their efforts. It doesn't mean that the person will do as well with your money as he or she did with the money of the person who referred you, but it certainly increases the likelihood.
- **Regularly and religiously review results.** Just because someone was referred to you doesn't mean you should relinquish responsibility for oversight of your account. Even if the person isn't intentionally mismanaging your money, he or she can make costly mistakes that negatively impact your acquisition of wealth.

- **Remember that you are the customer paying for a service.** Periodically step back and ask yourself if you're getting your money's worth in terms of expertise, work, and attention. Or are you settling for an occasional phone call and some confusing paperwork?

BOOKS

There are thousands of books related to financial planning that I could recommend. Certainly, many authors will look at this list and wonder why theirs isn't included. The reason is actually pretty simple. Since I couldn't include all of them, I selected books that were recommended to me that I took the time to review myself and books that I found to be personally helpful. Of course, I'd be acting like a "nice girl" if I didn't include my own book—so you'll find it tops the list.

Nice Girls Don't Get the Corner Office: 101 Unconscious Mistakes Women Make That Sabotage Their Careers, Lois P. Frankel, PhD (Warner Books, 2004).

Pay It Down! From Debt to Wealth on $10 a Day, Jean Sherman Chatzky (Portfolio, 2004).

If My Career's on a Fast Track, Where Do I Get a Road Map?, Anne Fisher (William Morrow & Company, 2001).

The Courage to Be Rich: Creating a Life of Spiritual and Material Abundance, Suze Orman (Penguin Putnam, 1999).

Feel the Fear—and Do It Anyway, Susan Jeffers (Ballantine, 1988).

Prince Charming Isn't Coming: How Women Get Smart about Money, Barbara Stanny (Putnam Penguin, 1997).

Secrets of Six-Figure Women: Surprising Strategies to Up Your Earnings and Change Your Life, Barbara Stanny (Harper-Business, 2004).

Women Don't Ask: Negotiation and the Gender Divide, Linda Babcock and Sara Laschever (Princeton University Press, 2003).

The Shadow Negotiation: How Women Can Master the Hidden Agendas That Determine Bargaining Success, Deborah Kolb and Judith Williams (Simon & Schuster, 2000).

It's More than Your Money—It's Your Life: The New Money Club for Women, Candace Bahr and Ginita Wall (Wiley, 2004).

She Wins, You Win: The Most Important Rule Every Businesswoman Needs to Know, Gail Evans (Gotham Books, 2003).

Play Like a Man, Win Like a Woman: What Men Know about Success That Women Need to Learn, Gail Evans (Broadway Books, 2001).

10 Smart Money Moves for Women: How to Conquer Your Fears, Judith Briles (McGraw-Hill, 1999).

Millionaire Women Next Door: The Many Journeys of Successful American Businesswomen, Thomas Stanley, PhD (Andrews McMeel, 2004).

Shacking Up: The Smart Girl's Guide to Living in Sin without Getting Burned, Stacey Whitman and Wynne Whitman (Broadway Books, 2003).

Why We Buy: The Science of Shopping, Paco Underhill (Simon & Schuster, 2000).

Home Based Business for Dummies, Sarah and Paul Edwards (For Dummies, 2000).

Your Money or Your Life: Transforming Your Relationship with Money and Achieving Financial Independence, Joe Dominguez and Vicki Robin (Penguin, 1992).

Ernst & Young's Financial Planning for Women: A Woman's Guide to Money for All of Life's Major Events, Elda Di Re et al. (John Wiley & Sons, 1999).

Ernst & Young Tax Guide, Peter W. Bernstein, ed. (John Wiley & Sons, 2003).

MAGAZINES AND NEWSPAPERS

Money
SmartMoney
Kiplinger's Personal Finance
Worth
Fortune
Forbes
BusinessWeek
Fast Company
Wall Street Journal
Divorcemagazine.com
Consumer Reports
USA Today

WEB SITES

Finance-Related

- **National Foundation for Credit Counseling**
  www.nfcc.org
  800-388-2227
  NFCC is the nation's largest and longest-serving national nonprofit credit counseling network. With more than one

thousand community-based agency offices across the country, NFCC members help more than 1.5 million households annually. NFCC members can be identified by the NFCC member seal. This seal signifies high standards for agency accreditation, counselor certification, and policies that ensure free or low-cost confidential services.

- **Institute for Divorce Financial Analysts**
  www.institutedfa.com
  800-875-1760
  The Institute for Divorce Financial Analysts (IDFA) is the premier national organization dedicated to the certification, education, and promotion of the use of financial professionals in the divorce arena. Certified divorce financial analysts are trained to answer questions and more for men and women in the process of divorce and to provide litigation support for their attorneys.

- **National Association of Investors Corporation**
  www.better-investing.org
  The National Association of Investors Corporation teaches individuals how to become successful strategic long-term investors. NAIC investors use fundamental analysis to study common stocks and mutual funds.

- **American Association of Individual Investors**
  www.aaii.com
  The American Association of Individual Investors specializes in providing investment education in investing basics, financial retirement planning, comparing mutual funds, stock market investing, and improving one's investment portfolio. AAII is a nonprofit organization that arms individual investors with the investment education and

tools needed to manage their finances effectively and profitably.

- **www.moneycentral.msn.com**
  Provides a variety of information related to investing, banking, and taxes.

- **New York Stock Exchange**
  www.nyse.com
  By clicking on "Education," you can find a number of free publications to help demystify the process of buying and selling stocks.

- **CNN Money**
  www.cgi.money.cnn.com/tools/networth.html
  This particular page at the CNN Money site provides you with a calculator to determine your net worth.

Low-Cost/Low-Investment Mutual Funds

ABN Amro Mid Cap Fund, www.abnfunds.com
T. Rowe Price Capital Appreciation Fund,
    www.troweprice.com
TIAA-CREF Equity Index Fund, www.tiaa-cref.org
Vanguard funds, www.vanguard.com

Charitable Organizations

National Database for Nonprofit Organizations,
    www.guidestar.org
Council on Foundations, www.cof.org

Child Support

National Child Support Enforcement Association,
    www.ncsea.org
Administration for Children and Families,
    www.acf.dhhs.gov/programs/cse

Comparison Shopping

www.mysimon.com
www.nextag.com
www.bizrate.com
www.pricescan.com
www.shrewd.com

Incentive Programs

www.bondrewards.com
www.babymint.com
www.upromise.com
www.edexpress.com
www.nesteggz.com

Other Useful Web Sites

National Do Not Call Registry,
    www.donotcall.gov or call 888-382-1222
Remove your name from mailing lists,
    www.dmaconsumers.org
Legal Zoom, www.legalzoom.com
U.S. Small Business Administration, www.sbaonline.sba.gov
Credit rating reports, www.myfico.com
Salary ranges, www.salary.com
Retirement calculator, www.choosetosave.com
A. M. Best insurance company ratings, www.ambest.com

Missing pension funds, www.pbgc.gov
Unclaimed property, www.unclaimed.org
Identity theft protection, www.consumerreports.org/main
Car leasing/buying information, www.leaseguide.com
Appraisers: *Antiques Roadshow,*
    www.pbs.org/wgbh/pages/roadshow

ONE FINAL THOUGHT

You've gotten this far. You spent money to buy this book (or at least someone you know did). If you're like most people, you took the time to complete the self-assessment in chapter 1. You spent time reading the book. And I would hope that you spent time thinking about how each of the mistakes applies to you. The biggest mistake you could make at this point would be to do nothing at all. The question I have for you is this: *What kind of return are you going to get on your investment?* Here's your first opportunity to show yourself that you're not just a "nice girl," but a smart woman.

I urge you to take the time to complete the action plan on the following page. C'mon. It will take no more than fifteen minutes—the amount of time you spend standing on line in Starbucks. Less than the amount of time it takes you to shop for a new outfit. It's up to you now. No one can make you rich—at least not according to my definition of having the amount of money you need in order to live your life free from concerns about money. It's something you have to do for yourself. Even if you take only one action, you will be one step closer to achieving your dream. Isn't that worth fifteen minutes?

ACTION PLAN

Whatever you can do or dream you can,
Begin.
Boldness has genius, power, and magic in it.
Begin it now.

—JOHANN GOETHE

WHAT I COMMIT TO DOING TO GET RICH	DATE BY WHICH I WILL TAKE THIS ACTION	RESOURCES OR PEOPLE I NEED TO HELP ME